STUFF I WROTE

by Rob Morton

For those that can see the humor in life and prefer to poke a sharp stick at it.

I realize the book is short but so is life. Enjoy both.

Table of Stuff

1. The Lemon Meringue Pie Adventure
2. Cat on a Long Thin Leash
3. Dangly Bits
4. 60
5. The Shed
6. A Bite of the Apple
7. Dam Nation
8. The Golf Trip
9. On the Occasion of My First M.I.
10. On the Occasion of My Second M.I.
11. On the Occasion of My Third M.I.
12. 8 Days in Havana

The Lemon Meringue Pie Adventure

So it's late in the afternoon and my daughter and I are loafing in the living room watching the food network. I can't remember the program exactly but at one point a lemon meringue pie appeared on it. As one we turned to each other and said "I want lemon meringue pie" in virtual unison.

It was close to dinner time which should have been a deterrent to us acting on our mutual craving but the lure of flaky crust, fluffy baked meringue and sweetly sour lemon filling was just too strong. We were overcome with lemon lust and needed a fix no matter what. "Let's go!"

We changed into appropriate clothing that could handle the damage that can be done during a lemon meringue feeding frenzy. Something that would shed the sticky filling and meringue. Something we could throw away later and hide any evidence of our shame. Where to go?

We live in a predominantly hipster, quasi bohemian neighborhood littered with young families. Hunting down the pie would not be an easy task. There were just too many trendy restaurants and healthy food choices available. We knew our task would be a challenge. We left the house quickly, salivating at the thought of success. It would be difficult but rewarding in the end we were sure.

Striding up the sidewalk toward Main Street, our hunting grounds, we spoke of the need for pie. We were giddy at the prospect of such a spontaneous satiation of a whimsical desire. This would be a good kill. A clean kill. One that would honor lemon meringue for some time to come. We sang of pie, sour lemons and sweet meringue. People stared and backed away as we approached. They could see the pie lust in our eyes and dared not be in the path of two such ravenous predators for fear we should catch the scent of a citrus perfume on their clothing or lemon zinger tea on their breath. We were focused and determined in our quest.

We reached the corner of 28th and Main and paused to survey the land. Where would we start? What establishment would provide our quarry? A restaurant or bakery or grocery store? We were in tough and we knew it. To our left and across the street lay a grocery store that advertised organic foods and healthy choices. Not likely, but never waste an opportunity. Organic lemons, free range eggs and whole grain flour could make a pie of dubious flavor lacking in sugar and fat but we would have to look none the less.

Before we crossed the street we ventured a stroll up to our left. There were two restaurants there that may be of interest. Never leave a stone unturned when searching out the elusive pie of choice. The first was a lounge type affair that offered appies and finger foods for patrons to wash down with a selection of local micro brews. The dessert section of the menu was sparse, offering fruit squares and other sundries not requiring cutlery to consume. Move on.

The next was a bistro affair with tables on the sidewalk where cappuccinos were sipped and biscotti was nibbled by diners trying to be too cool to be there. No luck. We crossed the street and headed for the grocery store sensing it would be fruitless but determined none the less. As we approached we watched the shoppers leave the store with brown paper bags and dressed in pork pie hats, long cardigans, vests and yoga pants. The smell of patchouli wafted across the breeze fortunately covering up the aroma of the two rummy panhandlers that perched on milk crates leaned up against the buildings with what appeared to be a baseball cap upturned in front of them. It could have been a small dead animal or an old crepe from the bistro across the street. A convenient location to beg as a liquor store sat next to our target.

Outside the store stood the usual array of wilting flowers and potted plants. A few bins of assorted fruits and vegetables beckoned shoppers to come in and make a purchase. These were not the organic varieties of course as those were much too expensive to leave out on the street and suffer the ravages of pilfering passersby. They were also much more waxy perfect than their organic cousins and as such made for a better display and marketing.

We entered the store and wondered over to the deli/bakery section first. There were sweets here. Tarts and tortes and squares and bars and even pies. But no lemon meringue. They had mint flavored Nanaimo bars and black forest cake. There was even a lemon torte and lemon tarts and a chocolate cream pie. The temptation to compromise was strong. A little whip cream on a lemon tart would be close to lemon meringue pie. They had red velvet cupcakes too and those would be a welcome surprise for my other daughter left back at home wondering where we had bolted off to. The chocolate cream pie would certainly provide a solid sugar fix and chocolate is always good. We searched about the rest of the bakery goods and passed on cinnamon buns and cookies and various fruit pies that for some reason all contained rhubarb, a dreaded ingredient of dubious flavor.

This was not looking good but we had a fallback position. We had a plan "B" should we not find exactly what we desired. Chocolate cream pie or lemon torte with whip cream would have to do should we fail. Something akin to a nicotine patch or methadone for a heroine junkie. We moved on.

Exiting the store, we turned left and headed down the street toward a coffee bar that serves desserts and gelato. Just maybe they would have a special on today. We passed our favorite pizza joint on the way and paused. They make a Roma style pizza that is "to die for" but come up short in the desserts department. The pizza is good. Very good and we are on the hunt. We will need fuel to sustain our hunt. Ok. Fine. One piece each but then on our way. I choose an Abruzzo with sopprasseta and mozzarella, my daughter has the Milano covered in prosciutto cotto and we share a slice of Trastevre with pancetta and pecorino. Fortified for our journey we say goodbye to Antonio and continue on the quest.

A few steps down the street and we come across a sushi joint that we order from quite often. In Vancouver it is difficult to walk even a half block without coming across a sushi joint or Starbucks for that matter. But this sushi joint makes some of the best and most inventive rolls in the city. Somehow, a Dragon Roll ends up in our possession. Tempura prawn with BBQ eel and avocado. It's good. It's not lemon meringue pie but it's good. Domo! Off to the coffee bar.

This is not one of your brand name coffee bars just a generic space habited by those that are too hip to go to Starbucks or Bean Around the World or Second Cup and averse to the corporate franchise culture. They cannot be packaged up with all those other folks that need their caffeine fix from a big box coffee shop except when they gather here and package themselves together in singularity. There is a freezer case filled with gelatos and ice cream and a bakery case filled with scones, muffins and croissant and day old sandwiches destined to become someone's Panini. There is nothing containing any lemon whatsoever except for the lemon sorbet. We grill the young woman behind the counter asking if she knows of any place nearby that may offer lemon meringue pie but her answers are vague at best and her most reliable suggestions are much too far away. There is a Reese's Peanut Butter cup ice cream in the freezer. Perhaps some of that will help to stave off the onset of depression at the thought of failure to find pie which is seeming to become imminent. One cup, two spoons please.

We sit dejected at one of the tables outside and eat the peanut butter and chocolate flavored frozen cream. It's pretty good. We make a note to stop in here again and try some other frozen offering but for now, we still must find lemon meringue pie. We hit the street.

We spy a Thai restaurant but not seeking mango or green tea ice cream we move on past three more sushi joints and a Tiki bar. We check the menus plastered to the windows of two more trendy hipster hangouts but there is no pie to speak of. Then we come across what might be our best opportunity so far. A design your own burger style diner thingy. Surely if you are going to serve burgers then you are going to offer pie as a final course. This makes too much sense. How could it be a miss? Alas, no pie. But a dynamite banana split. Take my word for it.

We wander several more blocks feeling aimless and worried that this may all be in vain. How could it be that lemon meringue pie had become such a scarce commodity? It was a staple for so long with the Tupperware set. We are sure it makes up one of the food groups on the recommended daily servings chart. This simply cannot be true. No lemon meringue pie when we are so desperately in need?

We begin to grasp at desperate straws and go in a halaal meat store, an East Indian food shop and a dollar store. I am beginning to shiver and break out into a cold sweat. My daughter is babbling incoherently. We are frustrated and angry and confused and consider staging a protest rally or a march on Safeway. How could this be? We are delirious with need.

We have reached our limit of endurance and are contemplating returning for the chocolate cream pie or lemon torte when we see what may be a beacon on the horizon. There on the corner at 25th and Main there stands what might be our salvation or very last option at least. A faulty neon sign that has hung there since the fifties and never worked properly from day one flickers out the name "Helen's Grill". A grill. Surely a "grill" would have lemon meringue pie.

We are buoyed by our discovery but remain tentative lest we be disappointed again. We cross the street and approach slowly not wanting to scare off our prey. Pies can be furtive creatures and prone to disappearing just as you reach for them. We stop beneath the neon sign and peer in the door. This is definitely a "grill". Worthy to appear as a "Dive" on Guy Fierri's Triple D. We can see leatherette covered booths lining the windows and a counter with torn vinyl topped stools that spin running the length of a laminate counter. Some potted plants are scattered about, spindly and striving for sunlight. It is sparsely populated by those seeking a good meat loaf, pork chop or chicken fried steak. Could this be it? Could this be our mother lode? Our nirvana? We open the greasy glass door and step in.

We are assaulted by the smell of a grill top and old deep fry oil. There is a large screen TV mounted up over the pass through window into the kitchen. The cook, a tall man with a pony tail, sits at the counter and stares up at the screen in spite of the volume being turned off. There is little conversation. This is a place to eat not dine or socialize. Some obscure 80's music plays in the background and there in front of us is a dessert case filled with pies. At Helens Grill there is no dessert other than pie and not a one contains rhubarb. Ice cream is available but only to be scooped onto the pie. Banana cream, apple, blue berry, raison, cherry, peach and of course lemon meringue pie. We had found it. It sat in the case and glowed with an ethereal halo. We had found our grail, our golden fleece, our fountain of youth. It had one piece missing and we could see that the filling was firm and the meringue piled high, fluffy inside with just the lifted tips turned golden brown. From out of the kitchen came a short middle aged Asian woman wearing slippers and a dirty apron. She swatted at the cook with a dish towel as she approached us from the other side of the counter. This must be Helen.

"Come in. Sit" she said in an accent that was just enough Chinese to be perfect.

"You have pie" I said stating the obvious.

"Lemon meringue pie" Georgia added for greater clarity of the obvious.

"Of course we have pie. All homemade" Helen told us. "What you want?" she asked.

"Lemon meringue pie" we said in unison and then explained our ordeal and the nature of our quest, how it all began and all its trials, tribulations and disappointments. She feigned interest but was happy to be the solution to our plight. We were prepared to fall on our knees and worship the dessert case but felt this would be misunderstood by her patrons.

She ushered us to a booth and we slid down onto the leatherette seats. There was the obligatory salt, pepper and vinegar as well as a bottle of soy sauce. There was also a small coin operated jukebox attached to the wall just beneath the window. The kind with the metal tabs across the top that flip the pages behind the glass containing a selection of hit songs that spanned the last 60 years or so. There was even some opera for the more genteel clientele.

We were quivering with excitement while trying to look nonchalant as we thumbed through the selection of tunes. Nothing stood out as appropriate to go with lemon meringue pie although one Roy Orbison song did come close. I looked around at the counter, the stools, the booth, the lethargic cook, the diners, the light starved foliage, plates and glasses stacked on shelves behind the counter and the booths each with their own juke box. I couldn't help but think that somewhere between the street and the seat we had slipped through a rift in the space time continuum and entered another place and time. Rod Serling was going to show up any second.

Our pie arrived with a rattle and slide as it hit the table top. It came with two glasses of water and spoons. This was magic. I hate forks. They have too many holes for things to fall through and you can't get punctured by a spoon should you miss the intended target. Yes, sometimes the train didn't quite make it in the tunnel. The glasses were clouded from too many trips through the dishwasher making the water look a bit suspect but a little did leap from them as they were plunked on the table. Some spillage is mandatory.

"You want coffee?" Helen asked.

I looked behind the counter and there sat a Bunn-o-matic coffee maker with a glass carafe sitting on the warmer. It looked like it had been there for several hours as the coffee was dark and reduced to the consistency of molasses elevating the caffeine content to the potency of methamphetamine.

"Absolutely" I said.

While Helen fetched the coffee swatting the cook once again as she passed we sat in silence and stared at our plates. This was the moment. We had finally come to the end of our pursuit. We had persevered and won the day. Somewhere off in the distance inside my head, the theme to an Indiana Jones movie played. The arrival of my coffee brought it to an abrupt halt. More spillage, contained by the saucer so that a drop would cling to the cup just long enough to fall on your shirt when you took your first drink.

Helen left and we picked up our spoons clinking them together in a toast and ate. There are few moments in life that bring true bliss. Climbing back into a warm bed on a cold night, finding the backscratcher to soothe that out of reach itch that you've had for the last hour, cuddling a puppy, having a good poop..... eating lemon meringue pie.

The filling was slightly tart, the meringue soft and sweet and the crust still flaky and not gone soggy from sitting too long. It was perfect. In that time and in that place it was perfect. It could have been nothing less.

We licked our plates clean and made sure there were no stray crumbs left on the table. Helen returned and I refused a second cup of coffee opting for sleep sometime in the next few days. We thanked her profusely and promised to spread the word to other pie hunters that Helen's was the place to find what you seek. We paid our bill, left a healthy tip and floated out of the restaurant.

The walk home was a blur. Returning from a spirit quest such as this leaves one a little euphoric and not necessarily in touch with reality. We talked of how good the pie was, the events of the day and most of all, the conquest. Life was glorious.

When we got home, dinner was served but we did not eat. We were full of pie.

Cat on a Long Thin Leash

So every morning I sit out on my front porch and have my morning coffee, with my newspaper, my laptop and most importantly, my cigar. I like cigars. Unfortunately, no one else in my family does and so I am exiled to the outdoors in order to enjoy one. I sit outside three times a day, every day, no matter what the time of year, the weather or the temperature. The porch is covered so I do not get wet and I have a little heater that blows warm air onto me when it is too cold not to be satisfied with my parka, blanket, fingerless mitts, scarf and balaclava. At times I resemble a terrorist Michelin man. I get some

One in particular fascinates me. He lives a few doors down from me and every morning, bright and early without fail, he takes his cat out for a walk on a very long leash. He does not hold on to the leash but rather lets it drag along the ground doing his best not to step on it which seems a bit self-defeating to me but there you go.

The cats name is Willow. For some reason I can't remember his. More often than not he wears gumboots like a Yorkshire sheep farmer. Perhaps he has a sheep on a leash that I have never seen.

Apparently, he has lost several cats to the coyotes that habituate our urban landscape and does not want to provide another meal to these opportunistic predators. I don't see a problem with that. Cats are cheap and considered a food product in many countries of the world. I don't like cats. They are assholes and should be categorized along with crows,

Canada geese, lamas and the people next door, all of whom are also assholes.

Cats are not pets, they are dictators and despots. They are self-centered, demanding, hissing and spitting little beasts with no regard for our mastery of this planet. We have several cats that wander the streets around here. I am not sure if they have human servants that feed them or if they are feral scavengers but they seem to hate each other and battle for turf in the middle of the night when I and my dogs are sleeping. This causes me to wake up and my dogs to go into a barking frenzy. Where are the coyotes when you need them?

I'm a dog man. Dogs are simple. They love you no matter what. Can you say that about your children or spouse? Test it out. Lock any one of your family members and your dog in the trunk of your car for two hours. When you let them out only one will be happy to see you.

I have another issue with cats and other pets for that matter. As a dog owner, I am required to purchase a license for my dogs every year. The money is meant to support the animal shelter. Last time I was at the shelter they were harboring a myriad of animals. There were cats, ferrets, various kinds of birds, assorted rodents and a lizard. Why am I required to subsidize these other animals? Why does a lizard get to freeload on my dollar? Lizards are also a food product in many countries. Put a license on that lizard!

So my neighbor walks his cat. On a leash that he doesn't hold on to. He is also convinced that the group of young people living between us are vampires. They have that certain Twilight look about them. One of the females does remind me of Wesley Snipes and you never see them out during the day coming and going only at the early hours of dawn or late in the evening. He may have a point. I think I will tear up my lawn and plant garlic just in case. I have a fountain that in future will contain holy water and I am melting down the silverware (or is that for werewolves?).

The vampires have a band. I use that term loosely. They have electrified instruments that they plug in, turn up and tune out. One of the guitarists does seem to have some chops but it's hard to tell above the cacophonous noise that rumbles out of their basement. I am sure that they torture the vocalist because he sounds to be in a great deal of pain. The drummer is clearly a demon or at least possessed by one. The bass player is learning to play on two strings now. Fortunately, no keyboard. The neighbors out back of them must be music critics because they throw rocks and bottles at the house whenever they practice.

The house itself is lovingly referred to by them as "The Hovel". I know this because I steal their Wi-Fi access regularly. The name is very appropriate. It's a rental. Belongs to a slum lord. Apparently the last tenants were gang members and it was a grow op before that. I guess we are moving up.

The front yard is surrounded by a 50's era wrought iron fence which has the primary purpose of containing the brambles and weeds that must thrive on bad music. Remember the studies that claimed plants grew better and healthier when they were played classical music? Well, ergo, weeds must grow better with whatever it is they play. I am sure the city would condemn the house if only they knew it was there. The boulevard is so overgrown the house cannot be seen from the street lending it that Detroit City look.

The backyard is another story entirely. I mean that. It deserves it's very own tale. Suffice it to say there is an eclectic mix of rotting furniture that surrounds the fire pit they have dug and on which they have been known to cook or sacrifice the odd goat. I have built a very tall and sturdy fence and taught my dogs to bark ferociously at the vampires whenever they wonder out. One of them has nun chucks that he flails about at imaginary opponents. Either that or he is serving penitence for his sins like that priest in The Da Vinci Code.

But my neighbor walks his cat. On a very long leash that drags along the ground. The cat climbs trees, chases birds and squirrels and wonders aimlessly through fenced yards filled with plants and bushes. He follows the leash as it winds through fences, around trees, shrubs, potted plants, up and down stairs and decorative garden art. Someday he will be arrested for trespassing or stalking or peeping tommery. The gumboots will get a few laughs on the arrest report. I think the cat is just being an asshole. I hear it laugh every now and then.

One morning he told me he found a dead squirrel on the boulevard. Figured it had short circuited the power lines by straddling two at a time. The carcass was still smoldering. Later in the week, I saw one fall out of a tree. For no apparent reason it simply plummeted from a branch and landed with a thump on the ground. This is something that squirrels don't do. Perhaps it was a failed suicide pact with the one that had fried itself on the power lines. It lifted its head and shook it as if to say WTF then ran at the nearest lamp post hitting it head first before trying to climb it. Their little claws don't cling so well to steel. The episode ended with a dog chasing it into the down pipe on a house across the street until a low flying crow caught the dog's attention and the dog ran off chasing it as it flew just barely out of reach of the dogs snapping jaws. It didn't bother to climb out of harm's way, it simply wanted to taunt the dog. Every now and then it would look back to see if the dog was still there and "caw" at it to keep the dog interested. Crows are assholes too. They disappeared down the street just as a frantic dog owner came running around the corner looking for a lost dog.

Oh look, there's a cat on a long loose leash. There's another cat, not on a leash, chasing the free end of the leash like it were a toy. It never gets the chance to catch it. Willow makes sure of that. Asshole. Here comes my neighbor, chasing the cat that's chasing the leash that Willow is keeping just out of reach of the other cat. They all stop abruptly as a squirrel comes out of a down pipe, runs out into the street and gets flattened by a passing UPS truck that doesn't even slow down. The pact has been honored.

My neighbor on the other side from the vampires comes out of his front door, I assume to see what the ruckus is all about but I realize quickly this is not his intention. He is wearing his best 70's Adidas shorts, you know the ones that are much too tight and short enough that the UPS driver should have stopped when he saw the package. He wears a bike helmet and a cycling t-shirt. No, not a competition shirt, one that advertises a bike maker (or a steroid producer, I'm not sure which). He's going for a ride. I tell him to watch out for falling squirrels and he gets this odd look on his face.

He's Dutch. I say this not out of any racial or cultural bias only that I think it is important. Every Dutch person I have ever met (and there have been three so I am an authority on this) has been "different". Comes from living below sea level I suppose. They are an odd people. He is an odd person. He likes to swim in cold water. I guess that's how he gets the shorts on. He shovels the snow from his sidewalk at 4:00 am while it is still snowing. He likes to skate on thin ice and I don't mean he likes to take chances, he skates on ice that is not quite thick enough. He owns a feral rabbit as a pet but it never leaves the house and poops in a kitty litter box. He uses the poop to fertilize his garden thus ensuring that his rabbit participates in the cycle of life without being eaten.

He takes a lot of pictures of flowers but none of them are tulips. He doesn't grow tulips. What kind of a Dutchman is that?

He parks his car by feel and has taught his sister-in-law to do the same which has resulted in my bumper being bumped far too often. When I questioned both of them after witnessing a crushing blow to my Volvo (they don't stop by the way, they continue to push expecting whatever it is that's impeding their progress to move) they both thought that they had hit the curb. I explained this was not so and would they please not damage my car any further. I even went so far as to give some kindly instructions on the correct way to parallel park. The last time I questioned him he told me that that is how he parks. He backs up until he hits something and then pulls forward much like a barge boat on a canal. By a miracle of self-restraint, I did not have him arrested for an act of public stupidity. Much to his credit, he later apologized after going on the interweb and discovering that his method of parking was considered careless driving and tickets could be issued or fines levied should a policeman in a bad mood witness the incident. He thought they were called bumpers because they were meant to be bumped. I told him to stop driving in wooden shoes. Dutch.

The cat on the leash watches the Dutchman ride away while the other one loses interest in the toy it was chasing and wanders off to inspect the tantalizing road kill. A dog owner comes by dragging his pet by the collar, a couple crows land in the tree out front and attempt a murder, my dogs bark viciously in the back yard and a squirrel drops from the sky.

The police have come by and stopped to question my neighbors. I see Willow smile and hear an evil chuckle. Somewhere, a Dutchman rides his bike.

Life goes on.

Dangly Bits

Disclaimer: I am not a Doctor. I am not a Scientist. I have no degree to back up my theoretical process. I have no process. I research life, think about it and make something up that fits my experience. I could be right or I could be wrong (couldn't imagine that). Basically, if you start with the assumption that I am full of shit, then 7 times out of 10 you will be right (now and then I get lucky or actually know what I'm talking about). **End of disclaimer.**

I believe that there is a common misconception in society that leads us to accept the concept that women have been dealt a tougher hand to play, what with childbirth, menstruation, menopause, discrimination, accepting the apple from the serpent, glass ceilings, high heeled shoes and see-through yoga pants. To this day, in many societies, women are property and subservient beings. There is a reason for this. Men are scared, always have been. If women should ever (and some have) discover the power of the male orgasm then the rolls would be reversed (which can be fun from time to time but not on a permanent basis).

While it may appear to be true that men have an easier time of it and tend to dominate, in truth men are in turn dominated to a much greater degree. Actually, we are all victims of how we deal with genetics and biological functioning but I will address that later. No. I wish to state clearly and categorically that women may not have it easy but men have it worse and it is time that we recognized this for the betterment of us all.

Men have been given the shaft. Literally. We have been handed the shorter stick of life (although we would all prefer a longer one). Women may have to put up with childbirth and hormones and monthly cycles and bad hair days but they do have the distinct advantage of knowing that, thanks to menopause, some of this will go away some day (excluding bad hair and a whole new set of emotional issues). No, men are stuck with their little albatross (size doesn't matter) from puberty to death. I speak, of course, of the PENIS (and attachments). These are the true leaders of men.

Before I give my reasoning I wish to first apologize to all women on behalf of all men for any and all unspeakable, unscrupulous, unthinkable, illegal, immoral, stupid and ludicrous acts ever committed by a man, on, to, near, on behalf of, or about any woman. This apology could be extended to certain domesticated animals as well but I have yet to hear any of them complain or file a law suit.

I'm sorry. Very, very sorry, **BUT IT WAS NOT OUR FAULT**! This is not meant to belittle or justify any unspeakable, unscrupulous, unthinkable, illegal, immoral, stupid and ludicrous acts, merely to say we can't help it and some of us (an arguable number) are more helpless than others.

The Penis and its related wrinkled attachment(s) (named after the Greek engineer Testichlese father of the modern jock strap) directly to the south of it are the beginning, the end and the root (sorry) of all male behavior.

What are these dangly bits and why are they so dominating? Why do men feel the need to check on them every so often and give them names and titles? Why is something so important to a man and so overtly sensitive just hanging out there exposed to attack or mishap (zippers being a prime culprit)? Any video containing a punch, kick or other blow to a man's groin creates a collective groan that can be heard around the world. I'm not sure that there is a female equivalent. Why would they want one?

It has long been believed that males are born with two brains; a larger one and a smaller but substantially more powerful one. Like the flounder's eyes one of these brains (the smaller one as size is an issue here), pushed along by hormones, migrates during the early stages of growth and lodges itself in the male reproductive organ like a symbiotic parasite and lies dormant until puberty when it raises its ugly head (so to speak). This is when males give up the option of rational thought.

It has been postulated that the male human body has only enough blood to operate one brain at a time. Ergo, if a male has two brains then only one can be functional and in control at any given moment. This is the basic problem.

When a boy reaches puberty he suddenly has a change of heart regarding the opposite sex that he has, up until this time, disliked and tormented to some degree. There is a welling up of biological interest that is hard to resist. His mostly boyish antics take on a different role in the need to impress or attract a young female which can be difficult with your pants constantly tented up like a yurt. Remember, it has a mind of its own and will do as it pleases which generally results in socially awkward moments for many young men.

It also leads to an interest in why it does this and how can one make the swelling go down, which Google or some cousin or friend is more than willing to teach you (explain verbally not show and tell or the hands on approach) if you haven't already discovered it on your own. It can involve long showers, afternoon "naps", study sessions or hiding in the closet.

Privacy becomes very important and is always interrupted at least once in every male's life by his mother (sister, aunt, nun).

This activity is not unusual in the animal kingdom. It is perfectly normal. Walruses, horses, penguins, monkeys, dogs and dolphins all do it as do squirrels (there's a joke about nuts here I'm sure) and porcupines (who do it very carefully).

The point is, it feels good. It is supposed to feel good. It releases endorphins and serotonin into the body and it brings down the swelling (if only temporarily). It can become an obsession in some young men leading to severe skin irritation, cramping, blindness, hairy palms and an afterlife of purgatory and damnation.

In the animal kingdom males are genetically predisposed to procreate. There is a deep drive to have sex as often as possible with any eligible or fertile female whether they want to or not. This biological necessity still exists in the modern human male, however, religious, legal and societal norms and morals dictate to what degree a man may act on these urges. But, that doesn't stop us from acting stupid.

In what has been a predominantly male dominated world throughout the ages the penis has taken on a mythical and glorified status resulting in the likes of the cod piece (where did they get that name), Japanese, ancient Greek and Roman festivals dedicated to the phallus, fertility statues so disproportionate that most men feel woefully inadequate, neck ties, various forms of architecture, speedo bathing suits and cylindrical fruits, vegetables or Charcuterie being stuffed into ones tighty-whities.

Our language has been infected by phrases and terminology related to the male organs. "Cock of the walk" and "Cock sure" being two examples (you may think that these sayings refer to roosters but I beg to differ). Imagine how anyone named Johnson, Jimmy or Willie must feel or any Richard who has had their name shortened. Use of the word "prick", regardless of context, causes young boys to collapse in a fit of laughter. You can either be a member or have a member or both if you happen to be an obnoxious golfer. There may very well be over two hundred words used to describe the penis (and you thought Inuit had a lot of words for snow). It is no wonder that we men have come to believe it is some sort of marvelous thing.

And why is this marvelous thing such an albatross? It makes us do things that in many or most cases make no sense. It can cause us to abandon a tried and true lifestyle to recapture our youth. It puffs up our vanity and egos. It leads us into temptation.

A shorter penis can create feelings of inadequacy and make a man go out and buy a rumbling muscle car, speed boat, motorcycle or monster truck. An older man ends up looking foolish while the younger one only attracts the attention of his compatriot males thereby defeating the purpose of the purchase. Sure, he provides all sorts of rides and excursions for a number of women but in the end the ride is short and unfulfilling.

A larger penis makes shopping for clothes very difficult. Finding the right pair of pants, shorts or banana hammock swim suit can be a fashion nightmare. When one wants the world to know that, "no that is not a zucchini", then how tight is too tight? Is blood flow to the legs really necessary? Conversely, the humble man may seek out looser fitting garments and risk the danger of bruising and contusions to the inner thigh, or casual exposure causing sunburn, finger pointing or a tranquilizer dart from an over-zealous reptile rescue group.

Size is an issue that men have wrestled with, emotionally and psychologically, since the first publication of Cosmo. In theory, it doesn't matter (at least that's what we like to believe) but the decision is still undetermined as the trial ended with a hung jury. Those that are less endowed may find it helpful to switch from imperial to metric measurements. It's a bit of a placebo but 10 cm sounds much better than the alternative. Then there's the whole length versus circumference debate but in the end a stump is still a stump no matter how big the tree was.

Yet another controversial issue is circumcision. Which looks better? Which works better? Why? What do they do with all those foreskins? Make wallets that turn into messenger bags when fondled? Is it a cleanliness issue or religious? If so, why not just dunk it in a bowl of holy water instead? Whoever decided that the best way to transition into adulthood was a close encounter between your penis and a razor blade?

Between males (other than gay men I presume) it is considered impolite to view another man's dangly bits. A men's bathroom is one of the few places (other than Jerusalem) where it is considered normal to stare at a wall and hold a conversation. An open shower room is fraught with potential social pitfalls and physical pratfalls as men attempt to shower with their eyes closed or walk while looking up at the ceiling. One must be very careful when lathering up as well. Best to use cold water at that juncture which leads me to wonder why nipples get bigger but the penis responds like a scared turtle in this circumstance.

Men are mostly driven by lust and a need to procreate. We try to avoid the procreation business if possible but mistakes do happen. Besides, who likes to swim with their socks on? This drive pushes us to greater heights of achievement (high blood pressure, high cholesterol) in the hopes of attracting an appropriate mate if only for a day or two. We are pressured by genetics to preen and groom ourselves to the same end. Advertisers have taken advantage of this predilection by showing us the rewards of using the right cologne or hair product as being a squadron of runway models that can't keep their hands off you. Apparently, drinking the right beer does the same thing.

We develop cheesy pick-up lines and dubious strategies (outright lying is not out of the question but a puppy works much better) in an effort to please our little despot. We will physically compete with other males to win the hand of some fair maiden. We will buy flowers or jewelry or cute little stuffed animals if required (when a shooter of Jack's just doesn't cut it). If desperate enough we will turn to writing poetry but this is always a last resort. We don't want to do these thing but we must.

As men grow older they make vain attempts to attract a female by growing "comb overs" to look virile which in a strong breeze will flip up exposing the naked scalp and fragile male ego while giving the appearance of a misplaced Mohawk on a head with no sense of decorum. If that shame reaches an unbearable level then toupees, plugs and weaves are resorted to resulting in a totally different form of social embarrassment and the extinction of several fur bearing animals. It's just hair. A peach with no fuzz tastes just the same as the fuzzy one. Personally, I've stopped wasting hormones growing hair and put them to better use.

Our dangling appendage will force us into fashion franchise stores for teenagers, sports car dealerships and romantic comedies at the local Cineplex (followed by a hard core action flick as a sort of purge). We will shop for shoes or handbags all the time avowing that, "no I don't mind missing the game". We will cuddle after sex and express our feelings. We don't want to do these thing but we must.

So needy is that second brain that we will artificially enhance its need and function long past its life expectancy by ingesting supplements, erectile dysfunction medication and in some cultures, poisonous or otherwise unusable animal body parts. We will do whatever is necessary to keep the little general standing.

This is the cross that we, as men, must bear. We would prefer it to be different (not really). We would much rather be in control of our own lives (even more so than we are now). We detest the control this dicktator (no typo) has over our lives (to a degree). None of us really wants to grow a comb-over.

60

Monday, August 4, 2014.

It is my birthday.

Today, I turn 60.

My dogs helped me celebrate it by waking me up at 5:23 am. They obviously felt that it was such an auspicious occasion that I should maximize the time available to celebrate. Very thoughtful. I particularly liked the panting dog breathe in my face followed by a wet nose in my ear and a severe tongue lashing as a wake-up call. I will not describe what that did to the dream I was having. I let them out just in time for an emergency vehicle to start up its siren and tear off to the scene of a crime, fire or health issue obviously caused by someone waking up and realizing they had suddenly become old. My dogs howled to ensure that everyone in the neighborhood was awake and prepared to mark the passing of my 6th decade. They are very considerate dogs.

It was much too early to get up so I went back to bed hoping to get a bit more sleep so that I would be able to stay awake through dinner. I lay there for a few short moments and realized I had to go pee. This would be the fourth time I had to do this since retiring the night before. Not an unusual occurrence for an older guy just an annoying one. As men (can't speak for women) get older, their bladders shrink or something else swells up and we can't hold it like we used to. This is a cruel joke of nature probably meant to give the old ones a chance to mark their territory while the younger ones slept off the party from the night before.

I went back to bed. Laying there I remembered the dream that my dogs had interrupted and smiled at the fact that, at least in my dreams, my virility and sexual prowess had not diminished with age. Then I became very disturbed by the fact that it had been my dogs that had brought that on. I will speak to my therapist about this.

I tossed and turned a bit trying to get comfortable. I have bursitis in my left shoulder and a pinched nerve in my right hip that causes my leg to go to sleep. I became jealous of my right leg. I believe that all body parts should sleep at the same time.

I suddenly realize that it is my birthday and I am turning sixty. I had forgotten. These things happen as you get older. You forget things. Like where you put your car keys, or what program you were about to open when you pulled up the task bar at the bottom of the screen on your laptop (recent occurrence) or your oldest child's name, which becomes quite obvious as you run through a litany of names of old friends, deceased pets and album covers from the sixties trying to recover from the faux pas.

But now I had remembered. It's my birthday. Perhaps if I just lay there a bit longer I will forget again and go back to sleep. Another siren wails, my dogs howl, the neighbors return home from an all-night binge, birds chirp cheerfully, a slight breeze sets off my wind chimes, two cats have an argument over territory and I have to pee again. I give up and get out of bed then promptly collapse because my right leg has gone to sleep. Happy Birthday.

I have a morning routine. A short stint in the bathroom and then to the kitchen which has large windows with no curtains opening up to the neighbors out back then I go back to my closet and put on some clothes because I have forgotten to get dressed and the neighbors have threatened me with a law suit should I cause any psychological damage to their children that play in their back yard.

Once appropriately attired, I grind my coffee or at least try to as I like dark roasted coffee which gums up the grinder and 2 out of 3 times results in me using my patented all-purpose coat hanger fix it tool to scrape out the clogged dispenser. After wiping the coffee grounds off the counter and sweeping up the beans I have spilt on the floor (very important if one my dogs eats them because the last thing anyone needs is a caffeine fueled Giant Malamute on the loose) I proceed to rinse out my 20 ounce stainless steel thermal mug (I hate cold coffee or going back for a second cup besides this way I can honestly say I only have one cup of coffee a day) that has just come out of the dishwasher with the sludge from yesterday's coffee still clinging to the bottom, rinse out my French Press coffee maker (my wife uses a Keurig but there is no damn way some machine is going to tell me how I like my coffee) and prepare my morning breakfast beverage of fruit juice mixed with ground up veggie powder and hemp fiber. Fiber is very important. I fill my kettle with water and put it on the gas stove (no electric or irradiated water for me) which has burners that emit a flame akin to the eruption of Vesuvius causing second degree burns from the overheated handle on the kettle when it is picked up and which you have once again forgotten about.

After running cold water over my charred hand, removing bits of melted plastic that had adhered to it, applying Polysporin and bandages, I don a heat proof glove and fill the French Press with water hot enough to scald my lips on the first sip (which it always does) and has six heaping scoops of ground coffee in it for my one cup of coffee which has the consistency of Heinz ketchup. I add four packages of sweetener in my cup (gotta watch the blood sugar) and a healthy shot of frankencream (fat free creamer for the cholesterol conscious) just to take the edge off the coffee.

I take the opportunity to step out on my back deck and wait for my youngest daughter to leave for work. She lives in the suite in the basement. I get a small bit of joy by being in the right place at the right moment to scare the living daylights out of my children. As she steps out her door and heads off I make an appropriate sound which has the desired effect. "Oh shit!" she says followed by some very disrespectful language directed at her father. I am elated.

I then check and delete my spam mail, select a cigar for the morning, (no day starts or ends without one) grab my laptop, tablet, cell phone and house phone, (technology is a burden) plus sundry other accessories for said technology and cigar and head outside (no smoking indoors) with my coffee mug dangling precariously from my little finger. Heaven forbid I should make two trips.

I set up camp on my front porch in the morning, back in the later afternoon and evening so as to stay out of the sun. It has nothing to do with UV rays or Melanoma, the laptop and tablet stop working when they overheat. On this particular morning, every single device required charging so I diligently plugged them into the three for one three pronged adapter because some items have three prongs and some have two prongs and all the multiple socketed extension cords you can buy at London Drugs have only two prong sockets and the ones with three prongs have only a single socket. Why? I used to cut off the rubber bit that was molded onto the end of the multi-tap extensions designed to prevent people from plugging in three pronged cords but a small house fire has discouraged me from doing that any more.

I then plugged the appropriate wire into the corresponding device. It is a known fact that all wires and cables have different connectors to provide employment for women and children in off shore manufacturing plants. No two devices have the same connector. Sure the USB cable was supposed to be universal, but only on one end.

I picked up my tablet to take up the daily challenge of Microsoft solitaire and noticed that the little light that indicated it was charging was not lit so I fiddled with it a bit then unplugged it and plugged it in again several times because we all know that if you do that enough it will magically fix itself. No luck. This made perfect sense because just the day before my power supply for my laptop had crapped out necessitating a trip to London Drugs (which is entirely the wrong name for a store that generates so much revenue from everything but drugs) to replace it and why not make a second trip today? I consider buying all of the cables and wires available so I won't have to go back tomorrow.

I curse designed redundancy, cheap manufacturing practices and Murphy's Law. A thing will only break down according to the need and desire of the user. The stronger the need or desire or time constraint, the greater the probability of malfunction. This law is exponential as well as the problem will escalate and be more complicated according to the need.

I check my other devices and note that none of them are showing signs of electrical input. I am suffering a total techno failure. It must be the breaker has blown. I locate my electrical panel and find no faults. I go back and ensure that the extension cord is properly plugged into the wall socket by removing and inserting it again several times (see above) and turn each device on and off again as this will certainly fix the problem. Again, no luck. I sit down and reach for my cigar that is resting in the stand alone ashtray directly above the three pronged adapter and extension cord that are not connected. I have forgotten to plug them together. I laugh to myself for a moment and then shed a tear for all the brain cells I had killed in the seventies.

Life is good again. All my technology is up and running. Thanks to my thermal mug, my coffee is still warm. My cigar has been chewed on a bit but is only moderately worse for the wear. I once again check my email (it has been more than five minutes and who knows what could have happened) and find I have received several wishes for a Happy Birthday. Thanks to all of those who have taken the time to remind me I am now entering my 7th decade.

I receive a phone call from my brother. He is an asshole. As am I. We only remember to call each other on our birthdays so that we have the opportunity to remind each other of the passing years and the ages we have acquired. Fortunately, he is **much older** than I am (take that you asshole) so at some point he will go senile and forget while I am still somewhat with it allowing me the opportunity to go one up.

I also receive a call from 1974. Some friends of mine were in Dawson City and had taken a photo of my signature on the wall of the dressing room I used in the Palace Grand Theatre when performing there and had sent it to me. It was right beside Burt Lahr`s (the cowardly lion). I was suddenly transported back 40 years in time although the memories were more than a bit foggy. I think that may be for the best. Running naked in public was quite popular back then and there was this thing called the Sour Toe Cocktail (don't ask).

Several of my neighbor's pass by and say good morning having no idea that I have suddenly become old right before their very eyes. I am certain that tomorrow there will be a rotting corpse sitting in my place having reached an age where this sort of thing can happen quite suddenly. I am sure they will all say good morning to my decaying body, pick up their dog`s poop in a plastic bag and carry on. We are an ambivalent society.

It may be obvious at this point that I am uncomfortable with the age I have achieved. Many people from my past would be amazed that I lived this long, I know I am. Given the abuses and excessive behavior of youth one can only marvel at the durability of the human body. The mind is a different story. I have become a bit unstable and prone to wandering. I plan to have a micro-chip implanted by my dog`s vet next week.

We have a tradition in our house that when it is your birthday you get to do whatever you like. There are certain restrictions of course. Mostly of them legally or morally based but for the most part the day is yours. I have opted for the hang around and do nothing approach in an attempt to fool myself into believing that this is not a significant event. It is no big deal, just another birthday. A different number in the age column of the sign in page of a restricted website. What's the difference? It's all in the marketing. If you list a product at $59.95 it will sell much easier than one marked $60.00 because it's not $60.00. Fortunately, I cannot be bought, I have my principals.

I play a video game on my computer. Nothing that requires quick reflexes, complex combinations of key strokes or too much thinking. I know my limits and am not prepared to test them. I avoid the sports genre as well as first person shooters and real time adventure/strategy sticking to role playing games. It is a rule I have adhered to in much of my social life as well.

I check the time and notice that it has somehow become mid-afternoon. I must have nodded off at some point. That sort of thing happens to the elderly. One minute you're enjoying a nice dinner with the family and the next you're face down and snoring into a plate of mashed potatoes and pureed peas. Not that much different than my early twenties now that I think of it.

It's a hot day and the sun has crept onto the front porch causing all my devices to cease functioning. I can't check my email, Facebook, Instagram, Pinterest or Twitter accounts. This is a crisis. I am officially out of the loop. My Farmville homestead will be full of weeds and moldering crops by now.

I quickly pack up all my worldly belongings intending to head for the back porch and cooler climes where, after an appropriate cooling down period, I can once again connect with the world at large. I will grab a couple ice packs from the freezer to speed the process up as withdrawal is setting in and I am beginning to shake and sweat. As I stand and head off I suddenly realize too late that I have forgotten to unplug the adapter from the extension cord. The ensuing techno-carnage is devastating. I weep like a small child on vacation that realizes it has left its favorite stuffed animal in the Motel 6 outside Boise upon arriving in Fresno on the way to Disneyland. This will require several trips to London Drugs and much pleading with my cell phone provider. I smile at the thought of acquiring new technology.

After migrating my SIM card over to an old steam powered cell phone I kept around for just such an emergency, I dismantle my desk top work station and set it up on the back porch. I will not be denied access to LinkedIn so I can update my skills page or connect with a Real Estate agent in Bulgaria.

I pour myself a cold beverage, light up a fresh cigar and watch my other daughter hose down our dogs. They seem to like it. The one is a bit difficult to hit with the spray because he found a few errant coffee beans and now resembles the artificial rabbit at a dog racing track. They express their thanks by shaking cold, muddy water over my daughter, myself and my redundant technology devices. There are a few sparks and sputters and the screen on my monitor needs a good cleaning but they somehow manage to survive the dog enhanced Tsunami.

After changing my clothes and some electronic fiddling about, I manage to log on and find that I have missed nothing. There have been a couple texts, a few more emails from friends passing on their best wishes for the day and my farm has not been ravaged by locusts. I reflect on this for a moment and think "could this be a cosmic metaphor on my reluctance to accept the inevitable? Is turning 60 nothing more than simply logging on to a different account to find that nothing has changed?" This is much too deep for me so I dismiss it out of hand in fear of elevating my blood pressure or aggravating some other age induced health issue.

My wife returns home from a retail therapy excursion, although I didn't know she had gone out (must have been while I drifted off) and has brought my daughter home from work with her. She is a pastry chef and has a cake for me with candles and a little white chocolate "Happy Birthday" placard. Having a pastry chef in the family is both a blessing and a curse. The blessing being that I have a sweet tooth the size of Saskatchewan and she brings home the mistakes and day olds from the bakery. The curse is I have a sweet tooth the size of Saskatchewan and a blood sugar level in the neighborhood of six figures.

I am treated to the requisite singing of" Happy Birthday" in all its discordant charm and receive three gifts as if the Magi have shown up having tracked down a star shining in the east and discovered it is merely the glow emanating from the plethora of candles burning on my cake. The "Gold" gift (from my wife) was a watch that I have coveted for many years now. In some respects and given that I was passing from one decade to another, it was akin to a retirement gift given to a long term employee. My wife was soon to become my ex-wife, thus the significance. The "Frankincense" was a fine Cuban cigar with a wonderful aroma that would see its demise later that evening. The "Myrrh" was a golf range finder with an adjustable eyepiece so that I could see through it without the need of my glasses to compensate for my failing vision. "Myrrh" is the expression I use when I have just missed a 2 foot putt for a par. I am grateful for the gifts and do my best to express my thanks while determining the distance to the neighbor's chimney and announcing it was time to get ready to go out to dinner. This was a fourth gift but it kind of spoiled the "Magi" metaphor so I didn't mention it.

"Getting ready" is a process, not just something I do haphazardly. It requires time, effort and planning. The proper attire for any occasion cannot be chosen at random. In my case it may be determined by what is clean, what needs ironing and what has a stain on it that I didn't notice before. Color and style coordination is important although I have managed to transcend the need for socks that match the outfit instead opting for a pair that would make Pipi Longstocking drool in spite of the white tie and tails.

Having options is very important when it comes to that final and disappointing look in the mirror (how the hell did that get there?). Clothing preparation can include taking the wrinkles out of two or three pairs of pants and a like number of shirts.

This can be done by either pressing them with a steam iron or hanging them in the bathroom while I have a shower. Then there is dealing with those annoying little marks that have shown up on your favorite shirt. A Tide stick, maybe some hand soap and water with a little scrubbing using your toothbrush will take care of that but will ensure a little time using my wife's blow dryer. I reserve at least an hour and a half to prep for any event. Packing for a trip is a nightmare.

Reservations have been made at an upscale restaurant downtown. I refuse to pay for Valet parking and find a convenient spot a mere half dozen blocks from our destination. I use my pay by phone app for the meter and discover that valet parking is $5.00 cheaper. We arrive fashionably late for dinner.

Our waiter has a thick French accent and the sommelier doesn't recommend any bottle of wine less than $200.00. I remain uncertain as to what the special was for the evening as I thought the waiter was coughing up phlegm when he described it so I didn't listen in an attempt to be polite. I do speak some French but my diction is suspect and the French are a bit touchy about their language so I refrained opting not to be tossed from the restaurant by an offended waiter.

Dinner was pleasant consisting of small talk interspersed with texting and checking on Facebook while posting a photo of every plate from every course on Instagram. There was the prerequisite familial sniping from time to time and a bit of "can you believe what she's wearing?" as the other clientele was surveyed. People watching complimented with unfounded judgement is a pastime we all enjoy.

After arranging a second mortgage on the house to pay for the dinner we took a cab back to the car and headed home. Our dogs were excited to see us but denied any immediate affection as we all ran about in an attempt to avoid being covered in Malamute fur. They are shedding and if you wish to wear the same outfit in the future without looking like an alpaca, then you avoid the dogs. There is also the slobber to contend with, but that is a different kind of social disaster.

It was late and after changing into dog appropriate clothing I retired to the back deck to enjoy the cigar I had been given (maybe check for emails and see how the farm was doing) while my wife and daughters had a last glass of wine and caught up on the latest episode of one of their favorite reality programs. This is a subject that I will not go into at this time as it requires a treatise that would make "War and Peace" look like a short story.

Each in their turn came out and wished me a final Happy Birthday and gave me a hug before retiring to bed. It was close to 1:00 am before I stubbed out my cigar and went in and lay down on the couch to watch a little television myself. My birthday was over. I was 60 plus one day. I woke up an hour and a half later because I had to pee. The television was blasting out the merits of the George Forman grill because I don't hear as well as I used to and had forgotten to hit the sleep button.

Nothing had really changed.

The Shed

So we sold the old house and bought a newer one. It was time to downsize and take a little equity out of our largest asset. The old house was just that. Old. It needed a lot of repair which required a lot of financial investment and a great deal more time invested on my own behalf. I am of the belief that if I can do a job adequately then why hire someone to do the work for you.

One of the criteria for the new purchase was that the house was to be in such a state that it required little if no effort from me to make it move in ready and comfortably livable. I had done a number of modifications and renovations to the two previous homes and did not want to get involved in anything more than lawn mowing and taking out the garbage. With this in mind and an inspection report in hand we made an acceptable offer and proceeded to move.

This turned out to be a task of monumental proportions. We had resided in the old place for some 23 years and accumulated quite a hoard of useless items spanning the growth of our two daughters from birth to adulthood. Every nook, cranny and crawlspace was jammed and crammed from stem to stern. It took me 3 months to sort it all out. It took 4 days alone just to go through the laundry room. We had no idea how many clothes we had. In the end, my wife lost all her socks and underwear in the move. The lesson is to not put clothes you wish to keep in garbage bags for moving.

I diligently set aside items for recycling, items for sale, items to be donated and items to be scrapped. As it turned out, most of the items for recycling, sale and donation could not be given away, sold or reused. The scrap pile was huge in the end. After all was said and done (donations picked up, garage sale complete and what could be recycled was sent to its demise) we ended up with two and a half tons that went to the land fill.

The worst and most depressing aspect of all this was that so much of what was thrown away was quite usable and in my day (good god I sound like my parents) would have been snapped up in an instant to furnish a young person's first apartment or been gratefully accepted by any number of reliable charitable organizations. But times have changed and barely cuddled stuffed animals or slightly used baby furnishings are no longer acceptable for fear of disease or lawsuit. Lawsuits have become a disease if you ask me. In the end we had to give away our baby grand piano to save it from being crushed along with the old house as it made way for a grander palace to be built in its place.

The move, not including packing, took 12 days in spite of hiring a moving company to take all the large items. It's surprising how the small things can add up. I had stuck to my resolve not to pay someone to do what I could do myself. This resolve has begun to fade. The physical and emotional payment exacted on myself and my family was never considered when deciding that this was something we could do ourselves. Some things are simply not worth the concept of clinging to pride.

So we moved.

As I have said, one of the criteria for our new home was that it would be basically move in ready. I was not that interested in being a host or subject of a DIY reality program. As it turned out, such was not the case. The home inspection revealed a number of niggling issues that needed attention along with some of more major import such as the roof replacement. Then of course there were the new design considerations that needed addressing. One could not simply live with what the previous owners had done. A new shower stall, granite counter top (which created the need for a new backsplash) and some cupboard alterations to provide more storage and accommodate the new fridge, arrived on my to-do list.

The new roof revealed some plumbing problems (yes there are plumbing things in the roof) which lead to some large holes in the walls that required repair along with the ones in the suite where a new electrical line was needed for the new dryer and dishwasher. This of course exposed some electrical problems that had to be dealt with while I replaced a number of light fixtures and bulbs.

We have 2 dogs a of very large variety and they reside in the back yard which was surrounded by an older fence which one of the dogs discovered could have panels knocked out if you jumped at it with both paws. A new escape route was opened once a week as I replaced the previous week's destruction. A new gate with a self-closing mechanism and an entire segment of fence that had to be moved forward beside the house to make room for the new storage shed was added to the accomplishments list. This last job came with a sense of foreboding and doom which I did not recognize at the time.

Then there were the bits and pieces of repair that had to be done following any move as well as all those little things that get neglected over the years by many home owners. Fix divots and scrapes left behind by the movers and paint them over. Align cupboards and replace broken switch plates. Glue down errant portions of door or window trim that has lifted away. Put things back into the holes they have fallen out of and generally replace all the worn and broken bits of appliances, drawers, door handles, shutters, etc.

By this time you may wonder why I have named this piece The Shed when I am going on about the move and the new house. The answer is perspective. As annoying and frustrating and ongoing and seemingly endless all these other chores may have appeared, there was one that stood out in its biblical proportion of trial and testing of patience and commitment. One that stood alone at the pinnacle of emotional and psychological endurance. One that truly went beyond the bounds of human capabilities and satanic torture.

The construction of a metal garden storage shed!

Here is a marvelous wonder of modern design engineering that would have won acclaim and lavish praise from Machiavelli himself. Spanish Inquisitors would have bowed down to its magnificence as a device of supreme torture. Sisyphus would consider his boulder a mere pebble and the act of rolling it a child's game in comparison to the construction of this structure. I wonder how bad and dysfunctional the lives of the designers must have been to exact this much revenge and retribution.

The design requirements must have been a challenge in order to create a structure of such flimsy and (no other way to put it) cheap materials. Is an eighth of an inch more on the length of a screw that much of a cost impediment? Could hiring someone who has graduated from elementary school to compile the instructions be too much to ask?

The first diagram of the construction process shows 2 people completing it and that is the last time we see the second person. This is neither a one person job nor a 2 person job as is suggested in the instructions. I enlisted the aid of my wife and daughter and felt I was short a talented craftsman, a journeyman welder, a mill wright and 3 assistants. I also ended up in divorce proceedings and will let you know the outcome of my child abuse case once I am released from the psychiatric hospital and recover from the myriad of lacerations. The shed now resembles the aftermath of a chainsaw massacre.

So horrid was this experience that I have jumped to the completion in order to avoid the reliving of the ordeal through the telling of the story. I will cease my whimpering and calm the quivering of my bandaged hands and get on with it.

The instructions might have well been written in Sanskrit and come with a qualified archeologist replete with Rosetta stone for interpretation. My head still hurts.

Step 1; level the sight. If you are really adventurous and are good friends with a cement finisher, you can pour a concrete slab on which to build your shed. This would triple the cost and send the aggravation factor through the roof but provide an excellent surface for the rust to adhere to as your monolith decays over the next two years. I opted out of the concrete pad and made the best of my sloping gravel driveway, piling rocks and debris in something that resembled a rectangle of the appropriate size and shape. It turned out to be more of a rhombus or parallelogram than a rectangle. (I'm glad I didn't waste my geometry lessons)

Step 2; assemble the base frame. This was the simplest step designed to lull the builder into a false sense of accomplishment. The only harbinger of what was to come was the undersized sheet metal screws that, once dropped, disappeared into the gravel never to be found. They later became described as suicidal screws. I am not sure if the screws merely did not want to be attached to this sort of project and thus leapt from my hand in an attempt to escape or simply perish rather than be applied to the structure. The magnetic tip on my cordless drill could not hold them in spite of the fact that it could have raised the Titanic if I could only get it down to where it rested. The other meaning of suicidal screw relates to a viable life option for the user once all the screws have either been lost in a sea of gravel or been stripped beyond usability. The designers had obviously anticipated that there might be a problem with their choice of fasteners and had conveniently provided enough to erect the Eiffel Tower which increased the delivery weight to the point that a crane was needed to lift the box from the truck.

Did I mention the washers that were to be applied along with each screw? Here was another stroke of shear genius. Of all the possible materials to utilize, the resulting decision was to rely on clear plastic washers. The advantage to clear plastic, of course, is that like a contact lens, it takes on the color and texture of whatever surface it has landed on. A perfect match for the suicidal screws. I suppose the washers didn't want to be seen in the same company.

What ever happened to nuts and bolts?

Step 3; erect the walls. Building the pyramids was a simpler task. This is the point in the instructions where the second person disappeared. A cruel joke. Imagine trying to stand a piece of paper on its edge in a 50kph gale. After an hour of deciding which panel went where and which panel it hooked up to, then catching them as they fell and ripped out the suicidal screws that I did manage to embed in the frame and hammering out the bends and folds at the bottoms and staunching the bleeding from the gashes in my hands caused by catching the bent wall panels as they twisted and flew like Dorothy's house in the Wizard of Oz, I gave up and pleaded with my wife and daughter to come out and help me. I think it speaks to my level of desperation, even at this time that I, a male of questionable testosterone levels but still holding on to a fragile ego, should ask for the assistance of female family members that have little or no experience in construction beyond assembling a casserole or dollar store diorama. To their credit (or possibly courage or stupidity) they agreed in spite of knowing my penchant for displays of anger, screaming and foul language laden with blame when inanimate objects will not do as I command. This would not be an exercise in family bonding. Eyeing my blood soaked clothes, they donned their least favorite outdoor clothing and came to my rescue.

The ensuing scene would have made the likes of Charlie Chaplin, the Keystone Cops and the Three Stooges weep with jealousy at the novel congruence of comedy and pathos. Envision my wife and child attempting to secure four corners of a paper thin sheet metal building whilst I was alternating between stripping cheap screws, crawling on my hands and knees searching for the suicidal fasteners (more cause for blood and scars) and telling them in no uncertain terms that they were doing everything wrong (they weren't but surely it wasn't my fault). In no time at all (roughly two and a half hours) we had the walls more or less in place. This, just in time for the rain to begin and the wind to elevate to hurricane strength.

Step 3; bracing the walls. This is a relative term. The term bracing normally implies adding strength. In this case, bracing means applying and removing several shaped pieces of metal that all look alike yet must be carefully arranged in place so that all four walls will fly off or fall down as one. The committee process of deciding which piece went where made the US government look positively functional. In spite of the filibustering, we managed to brace the walls both at the

47

center and across the top. At this point, noticing that my Daughter was in tears and my wife was toying with a razor knife, I took the bold and perhaps wisest step and released them from their obligation to assist me. From here on out I would suffer the torment alone.

Step 4; the roof. Again, a relative term. It was indeed a roof in that it covered the shed. Heaven forbid that it should hold out the rain or support anything heavier than itself. A light hail storm would render it useless. Once more I was challenged by another rubix cube of assembly. It was getting dark. The few hours that I had allotted as suggested by the instructions had long since passed. I labored on, wearing the job of construction like a hair shirt. I would finish but not before I rested my hand on the roof to steady myself on the step ladder and promptly bent the piece into a lovely and large sheet metal "L". I reacted in my usual manner and slammed my drill down on another piece of the (expletive) roof so that I could have a matching and complimentary pair.

Fortunately, I enjoy watching DIY programs and had retained enough of what I had seen that I could repair the fender of a late model Ford that had been driven into a concrete abutment. Repairing the roof was no match for my skills and only required a small amount of "bondo".

Step 5; adding the decorative trim. This was not so much decorative trim as something to cover the sharp edges with something a bit blunter so that concussion was a sound possibility but blood loss would be minimal. This turned out to be a fairly simple step and buoyed my enthusiasm for the chance of completion. Foolish.

Step 6; hanging the door. The door or rather doors were to be hung from a track at the top and inserted into a trough at the bottom so they could slide open and closed. This required some rails and rollers and other sundry hardware that could be assembled in an amazing array of incorrect configurations. Like Edison, I discovered a thousand ways to fail before I succeeded. I was working by flashlight now. It was close to midnight I'm sure. The torture was ending and I could soon rest from my ordeal. Karma would owe me big time after this.

Step 7; the floor. Are you kidding? Apparently, you could add a floor but preparations should have been made in step one or two. I could see where the gravel I had built my edifice on would not be the best surface for items with wheels. Also, there was a good chance that the debris and rocks I had used to level the structure would be forced out causing a catastrophic failure. This is when calamity turned to fortune. My fence was a bit old and more than a bit flimsy and my dogs had discovered that if they pushed hard enough on it, the panels would fall out. They discovered this at 6:00 am on Christmas morning and had gone "walk about" for a while. After repairing the fence (thanks Santa for the cedar) I had kept the old six inch tongue and grove pieces meaning to send them off to the dump at a later date. I retrieved them and laid them riff raff across the gravel inside the shed. I was done. Tomorrow I would fill it with all my implements of weed destruction and lawn circumcision. I cleaned up my tools and assorted left over bits and pieces. (no extra screws) I was done. Pride swelled up in my chest and I was overwhelmed by a sense of accomplishment. I had beaten the devil. The beast was tamed. I stood and admired my handy work under the halogen construction lights with a smile on my face and blood on my hands. I stepped forward and slid the doors closed then went off to the emergency ward as I was feeling a bit faint.

That is the story of my Heart of Darkness. My Old man and the Sea. My personal struggle of good against evil. I could rest and be at peace for I had won.

To this day there is nothing in the shed. I cannot get the doors open.

A Bite of the Apple

It is my daughter's 25th birthday and we're going to New York. The Big Apple. The city that never sleeps. This trip has been in the planning for 3 years now. The anticipation is palpable. The excitement is building and the countdown has begun. The research has been done, lists compiled and a plan of attack is imminent. I hear about it daily. NEW YORK!

Day 1: The journey begins.
Our flight leaves at an early hour but security makes it totally unreasonable. Nothing like arriving 90 minutes ahead of your flight so you can hang around your gate for an hour waiting to board. Worse, I am incapable of operating the kiosk for U.S. customs. They let us in anyway.

We kill time with an airport crusty egg breakfast and what appears to be deep fried bacon finishing just in time to get to our gate for boarding. There are children. Lots of them. Why would anyone take children to New York? Specifically on our flight.

Our zone is called and we head down the gangway and onto the plane. Finding our seats we are deflated to see that we are seated one row ahead and across the aisle from a cranky young child. The father is trying to calm the urchin with a very annoying toy that emits a nerve rattling grinding sound. Perhaps the child is a Klingon and finds this sort of thing soothing. Seated behind Georgia is something that likes to pummel airline seats. Not a good start.

We trundle out to the runway and take off. Amazingly, the child becomes calm. Dad gave her a shooter of Benadryl I'm sure. The flight is mostly uneventful other than Georgia being bounced forward every now and then. The Captain finally announces that we will be making our decent into Newark but due to strong winds he expects a little turbulence. A true master of understatement. I have been on rollercoasters that had a more gentle ride.

For whatever reason, the decent into Newark requires a great deal of turning and circling about which prolongs the whole landing process. Not usually a problem unless you are riding a wild bull with wings. There was much clenching of teeth (and other things). The plane was quite silent other than the sound of a few prayers being mumbled by those more religious than us. We were trying to look cool while reaching for the airsick bags. I could have sworn I heard our pilot laughing maniacally as the cabin crew collectively kissed their asses goodbye.

After what seemed like an eternity of bare back bronco busting we hit the runway.....and bounced. It's a good thing that we bounced because I'm sure we were at a very acute angle in respect to the tarmac that we were to decelerate on. We hit the runway again at a much better angle of attack having been straightened out on our first hit. A couple more hops and the front wheels made contact. We were down.

It's not unusual in these sorts of circumstances for the occupants (or survivors) to applaud the prowess of their captain. Our group was silent. Having stared death in the face it seemed inappropriate to provide an ovation. What could be worse?

The Newark airport. Touch nothing. Try not to inhale. Do not make contact with the seats in the bathrooms. Wear a body condom if you can. The only thing that surpassed the uncleanliness of the airport was the inability of anyone to provide service. Not to mention that lineups are meant to be ignored. It takes 3 people and 20 minutes to confirm a shuttle reservation.

Finally we end up on board a shared shuttle bound for Manhattan. First we must travel through New Jersey. Not a pretty sight. I will refrain from comment on New York's ugly cousin.

Our driver is aggressive to say the least. After a harrowing landing there's nothing that calms the nerves more than a crowded van being driven by a man with a death wish. Perhaps it was the 3 toll booths that we drove through at slightly subsonic speed that put him off. Or maybe it was the constant gridlock of Manhattan traffic that pushed him over the edge. I'm sure he heard voices in his head because he kept speaking to himself as he drove alternating between full throttle and full brake while all the time honking the horn. The object of driving in New York appears to be seeing just how close you can come to other vehicles when changing lanes or applying the brakes without ever making contact. Mirrors are meant to be ignored.

We were the second drop off. Thank god for that. As we left the van the look on the other passengers faces said "please...take us with you....save us from this hell". We ignored them (as any good New Yorker would), accepted our baggage from the driver, wished him all the best with his and headed into our hotel.

We are staying at the ROW hotel. It has just been renovated and it looked pretty good online. Updated to attract a younger crowd with sort of a post-industrial feel. The lobby is rocking. It's full of people and the music is loud. Looks a bit like a disco hotel. Or a strip bar. Can't decide. I'm sure they have a mirror ball somewhere. There is always a lineup at the check in desk. At times it is massive.

We approach the desk to check in and there is an argument ensuing between an employee and a guest who wants to speak to a manager. Apparently the guest felt he had been screwed over when the employee had offered a better deal just to be a nice guy. Of course this is New York so it all has to be completed by yelling across the room at each other. The guest wanders off just before the manager shows up. We check in and Georgia manages a couple comps for drinks in the bar.

We head to the elevators where you push a button and the system assigns you an elevator. Strange. We only travel in the F, G and H designations while we are there. In the elevator, the music is loud. It is not what you expect to hear on an elevator. Rockin' lobby……rockin' elevator.

We exit the elevator and head to our room. I use that term loosely. Opening the door we are treated to a very spacious closet. If this is a superior twin then I would hate to see an inferior one. There is not enough room to change your mind let alone your outfit. The photos online were well composed. Our luggage is delivered and the bell hop seems astounded that we would tip him. After several tries we arrive at an arrangement that allows us to access our luggage but not the bathroom. We rearrange and are left with about 6 square feet of floor space with no access to the closet (yes there was a closet) but could get in the bathroom and our beds. We manage to get changed and head out into the streets of New York. There is nothing to rival the sight of Times Square at night. It is always filled with people and neon and lights and advertising and cops. Cops everywhere. Many in full out attack gear. The naked cowboy is absent which I find disappointing but there are a number of animated characters and the obligatory Statue of Liberty available for photo ops. There is also a drummer with an assortment of plastic buckets and kitchenware that is more of a musician than most rock bands have. Amazing.

I am travelling with Georgia. She is an attractive young thing and I an older gentleman. Funny what perceptions that engenders in passersby. You can see it in their eyes. The way they look. The number of times they look between her and I. He must be wealthy. She is an escort. He's a pimp. She's a gold digger. You can read their faces like a newspaper. We counted over 40 "looks" during our stay. This does not include any gay men attracted to bears or lesbian women. They only looked at either myself or Georgia. Perhaps the most interesting encounters of this type occurred on our first night. I was a white man dressed all in black with a young woman at my side. We passed a black man dressed all in white with a young woman at his side. He smiled, nodded, winked and touched the brim of his fedora as we passed each other. A moment never to be repeated, I'm sure.

We wander about looking for a place to eat and finally settle on a saloon on 45th St. It looks pretty classic and like many Manhattan establishments, it has two stories. We are seated upstairs in a booth. Our waiter arrives and Georgia orders a Manhattan. You have to. He returns and we discover that he is a surfer dude from Socal. San Diego. Throughout our dinner he spends more time talking with us than serving other patrons. He turns out to be a highlight of our trip.

We order a combo appetizer platter that provides the best and worst from the appetizer menu on one plate. The chicken tenders could have been used as cobblestones but the mozza sticks were quite good. Our entrees came with mashed potatoes that could have been used to apply wall paper. The veggies were all but cooked. But the meat was fabulous. We decided not to chance dessert here and went out in search of a pastry shop.

We found the renowned Cake Boss's shop and went in. It was crowded and there were no numbers left to dispense ensuring an orderly queue. There were too many imperfections for Georgia for us to stay or order something. We find another shop a half block away that was empty and go in. I order a couple canoles (fresh filled) and Georgia gets a cupcake. We head back towards our hotel and indulge in our sweets. They were sweet. Beyond sweet. My teeth screamed in agony as I tried to enjoy my much awaited canole. They remained unfinished as we returned to the rockin' lobby, the disco elevators and our sleeping closet. Good thing you spend most of your time in your hotel room with your eyes closed. We share a laugh and promise to make the best of all of it no matter what. Good Night.

Day 2: It's raining in NY.
It's pissing rain. It's also cold. We check out the view from our room and are treated to brick walls and a tarp strung between the buildings that is covered in garbage thrown from the surrounding windows. We have a clear view into several apartments.

In a room this small it is important to get out. You can't help bumping into each other. Literally. It's more like a dance routine. Side step, shuffle and turn. Time for breakfast. We venture out and enter the elevator. Where most elevator music is annoying in its attempt not to offend, our elevators assault your senses challenging you not to dance while you descend to the lobby.

We choose a place close to our hotel that looked promising. Again we are seated upstairs. We order and receive plates of food that would overwhelm a family of refugees. If size matters then it was great. If taste is your concern then fail. Do these people not know how to make a cup of coffee? I look out the window and see a zombie crossing the street. It turns out that New York is full of mythical and legendary creatures. Later I encounter a hobbit, two trolls and several witches.

It is a lousy day so we choose to go to a tourist landmark and head to the museum of modern art. On the way we discover that unlike Vancouver there is no umbrella etiquette in New York. There are however a number of buskers selling umbrellas. There are buskers everywhere. They rival Bangkok with their attempts to sell you bus trips, comedy shows, theatre tickets and their sister. I notice several people bleeding from umbrella wounds on their heads and faces. One umbrella salesman notes that Georgia is "sweet like sugar and will melt in the rain".

On our way to MOMA we encounter a problem which will plague us for most of our trip. We get lost. I have been to New York several times but have always stayed on the other side of Times Square. Everything is backwards. On our way we come across a Christmas store. I buy three tacky ornaments for my tree. One will get broken on my way home. Georgia gets one for her mom and one for her boyfriend. We sing Christmas carols in April. The staff hate Christmas. We leave.

We begin to wander. We walk in the wrong direction several times. Where is MOMA? In spite of Georgia's protestations I go against all male instincts and ask for directions. We find MOMA. These people know how to organize a line. We are impressed.

MOMA was impressive for the most part. The first floor was dedicated to art that depicted the degradation of society. Very moving. The second floor had a lot of model Japanese architecture and modern industrial concepts. Georgia gets in trouble for sitting on an art work. To be honest, I would have sat there too. Interesting but not thrilling. The next two floors were dedicated to art and design from the latter half of the 20th century. This is when we discovered that we should have started from the top floor. Interesting but I lived through it so...... The next floor was full of people and impressionists and post impressionists. Monet, Gaugin, Picasso, Dali and the list goes on. Wow. The next floor is a Degas exhibit. I think he was seriously depressed. Too many people. No decorum. We leave.

Amazingly we manage to find our way to our next target, Rockefeller Centre, dodging umbrellas. Walking in New York is a challenge. No one gives way. Best to just put your head down and walk. If they move....fine. If they don't.... hit them. Never say excuse me or sorry or pardon me or whatever. I'm walkin' here!

New York converses in a few ways. Quiet if you are friends, loud if you are in dispute and by horn if you are driving. Have no qualms to be expressive. They understand. They will not be offended. They will also not look you in the eye. They look to the side or above or beyond or through but not in the eye. It's like you might catch something if you actually meet eye to eye. Strange as I have often found New Yorkers to be quite friendly when you actually talk to them.

As we walk it becomes obvious that there are cops in front of every hotel. There are police everywhere. They are wary. They scan the crowd. They are scared. Are the terrorists winning?

Georgia has told me that this trip was not about shopping. Then we hit the Lego store, the Nintendo store and the Disney store. Both Lego and Nintendo were at the Rockefeller center. Lego was mild. Not too serious. Nintendo was Geek central. OMG. Nerdana. She was nuts. Overloaded. Apoplectic. A weeks wages for most people and we managed to get out. All her gamer friends had gifts. Then Disney and all the little princesses. I'm dying. Googaws and thingys and all sorts of stuff that I'm sure will thrill her friends and family but......

We go back to our room. Georgia is thrilled. I am exhausted. We nap.

It's time for dinner. On 44th we had discovered an Italian restaurant that looked interesting. As it turned out, 44th was a lucky street for us. We get prepared for dinner and head off to Ostaria al doge. We only go a couple blocks out of our way before getting on track. The restaurant is wonderful. Who needs reservations?

The show for tonight is Chicago. No sets. No costumes. Just singing and dancing. Pure Broadway. Excellent. Georgia gets a drink and is told that nothing goes better with homicide than red wine. She also gets in trouble for leaning on the stage. At intermission she gets a double delivered in line to the women's washroom with a small tip. Her father's daughter. Amazingly they have vendors in the aisles just like at a baseball game. Wine, water and candy delivered right to you seat.

The show is wonderful. Afterward we go to a dive bar we found on 44th, Jimmy's Corner. God but it is perfect. It is owned by Mohamed Ali's trainer. Dollar bills hang behind the bar. Colored lights decorate the walls. There are boxing photos everywhere. The clientele are all local. The ambiance is perfect. This is New York. We meet and talk with a guy from queens and a couple from midtown. Too good. Its midnight and time to head back to our little room. And to bed.

Day 3: A Better Breakfast.
The title says it all. We found a small bistro on 45th that served decent coffee and a breakfast that was pretty good. It's a nice day, sort of. The sun is shining but there is a cold wind. We are planning a trip to the central park zoo. We hit the streets fortified and prepared for a good day. Some 7 blocks later we discover we have been once again heading in the wrong direction. If we only had a compass. In the mean time we got thrown out of a park because I was smoking a cigar. Georgia remembered that her grandfather gave her a key chain compass. We never get lost again.

We head uptown to the zoo and masses of children. It is spring break. There are gaggles of girls and bunches of boys everywhere. What ever happened to Cancun as a destination? On our way and many times on our ways we stop at pastry shops. I would eat more pastries in these few short days than I would eat in a year. There should be some sort of tax deduction for travelling with a pastry chef or insurance for subsequent hardened arteries.

We wend our way past a plethora of hucksters, New York beautiful people and mythical creatures. It becomes obvious that traffic lights are merely a suggestion for pedestrians should you ignore them however you do risk becoming a target. At one point we come across a truck driver that tells a cop on the corner to "fuck off" because he is "being an asshole". The cop wanders off. God it's cold. Georgia buys a toque (commonly and improperly referred to as a beanie). Generally a fashion faux pas but not now.

We get to the zoo. The best deal in town. Not really much of a zoo. We can see most of the animals with a drive up one of our provincial highways. Harbor seals and Grizzly bears are a bit ho hum. We did see a grizzly that looked a lot like my dog Thor. Not sure what to make of that. But there was a snow leopard and some interesting ducks in the tropical exhibit that made it worthwhile. There were also a number of very young children on field trips. One poor kid was suffering from dysentery and vomiting on a regular basis. We could only feel bad. She felt worse. Georgia bought yet another gift.

We bow our heads to the wind and head down 8th Ave looking for food. Approaching a corner she says "let's go there" but walks past the initial point of interest as if that's what she intended and we enter a whole in the wall Chinese noodle joint. The walls are lined with pictures of food celebs that have honored this venue. We order too much food and it is delicious. We get warm. We take some home to join our sweets from the other night. We brave the cruel cold streets of New York and head back to the rockin' lobby. We dance in the elevator and then we nap.

Tonight we see Kinky Boots. The other end of the spectrum from Chicago. Lots of costumes and sets and production numbers. Georgia works her drink magic and ends up with double vodkas pronto before the show and at intermission. The drag queens steal the show. In particular the young black man that plays Lola. He is FABULOUS! At the end the audience stands. We are reluctant. Very good but not worthy of a standing ovation. It has become too common to stand and applaud. Have some standards people.

After the show we head for a late night dinner at a New York icon, Sardi's. Once the place to be and the place to be seen Sardi's is not what it used to be. Classic red booths and caricatures clad walls with red vested servers and a very attentive maitre'd. There is a scant and older crowd. It is not quite what it used to be. The food is ok for the most part although their signature dessert is bad. The service is mediocre. Unfortunate. Like a dying royal. Too bad.

Back to our little home.

Good night Day 4: The Long Journey.
Finally a decent breakfast and a good cup of coffee. Just what's required for the journey we have planned for today. We are heading south through Soho, Little Italy, Tribeca, China Town and the financial district. A walk of some 70 to 75 blocks.

Georgia investigates several pastry shops while I wait on the street smoking a cigar. None of the passersby meets my eye. Not even the hobbit.

We reach the fringe of Soho and suddenly Georgia is struck with the overwhelming urge to purchase retail goods. We have found the realm of the elusive boutique shop. A couple more gifts, an éclair, a blouse, a skirt, a pair of shoes, a jacket and another pair of shoes in Little Italy. I stop and pat every dog we come across going so far as to go in a shop to accost a white husky. I am having fur withdrawals.

Exhausted from spending copious amounts of cash, we stop at a restaurant that was used as a location in The Sopranos. Great pizza and a classic ambiance. Georgia still had some money left so we departed for China town and other environs.

We come to the conclusion that once you have seen one China Town or Night Market you've pretty much seen them all. Anywhere. The weather begins to turn and the wind picks up. We consult our compass and Google maps and speed up hoping to reach Wall St. before Dorothy's house drops on us. Leaving a sheltered park we arrive on the open streets and come full face into the gale. It is brutal. I lose my hat and chase it down the street. It is returned to me by kindly woman whose ankles were bruised when it hit her. I hold it down with both hands saving my scalp from frost bite. Georgia is saved from being blown away by the weight of her numerous purchases.

Undaunted, we plow into the storm that has become an arctic squall. We are explorers in a wild land. Adventurers seeking the Holy Grail. Another block and our daunt is gone. We hail a cab and head back to the hotel changing lanes every 100 meters and honking all the way. This is one of the prime forms of communication in New York. The other is to yell at the other person for whatever reason suits your purpose. Preferably from a distance. The other person is optional.

Reaching our hotel, we elbow our way across the rockin' and lobby and refrain from dancing in the discovator. In our room we turn the temperature up to medium rare and climb under the covers of our respective beds to recover from the hypothermia. Afterward, there is a fashion show before we head out to dinner.

We have decided on a steak house for our final dinner in New York. Something special. Fearing any further frost bite or damage from flying debris, we choose the closet steak house we could find. The West Side Steak House on 10th Ave. Our hotel is on 8th Ave. We head west and cross 9th Ave. We pass The Actors Studio and begin to realize just how unusually long this block is. Something has changed. It is quiet. There is less traffic. No advertising or neon. No tourists. We have walked through a tear in the space, time continuum and come out in a different New York. A parallel universe. One block and the world has changed.

The restaurant has the feel of an old time steak house. Wood on the walls and white linen on the tables. Classic standards are playing on the sound system. At one point we sing and dance in our seats to The Girl from Ipanema. The waiter tells us we have to stop because they do not have the cabaret license required in New York for that sort of activity. He is joking. There is a family here and some friends that have met for dinner after work. A woman comes in and is seated in the back at a table for two. You get the feeling this is her table and she is a regular patron. No one ever occupies the other seat.

Dinner is all we expected including the complimentary cake and signing of Happy Birthday. Well-cooked and seasoned meat. Crab cakes that were more crab than cake and cocktail sauce in a gravy boat. No starchy potatoes. Georgia finishes with a fine 18 year old scotch. We leave and cross 10th Ave. into the portal that will take us back to our time and place.

We stroll back to our hotel and entering the doorway it is obvious that the rockin' lobby is rockin' a bit harder. The music is loud and not so discoish. There is a larger than normal crowd. We climb the stairs and round the corner into the bar and low and behold there is a live band playing. Who knew? They were pretty good too. They claimed to be an R & B band but I would argue that point. They were eclectic. Musicians dropped in to play some songs and a waitress sang as well. The lead singer, Timatha, was very interactive but she was surpassed by the nerdiest looking trombone player I have ever seen. I think I recognized him from the Nintendo store. They both wandered through the crowd as they sang or played to the point where our friendly trombone player got a little too interactive with an inebriated, blond BBW and they both ended up sprawled on the floor. His attempts to be interactive with Georgia were just about as successful. The rockin' lobby had only partially redeemed itself.

We sat at the bar next to a couple from St Louis. They were quite friendly and in New York to celebrate her sister's birthday. Seems to be the thing to do. For some reason she recognized me as an actor. When asked what I had appeared in I mentioned The X Files which sent the bartender into an Oh My God moment. He had every episode of it at home. The husband had an interesting life and ended up in the Marines. He spent three days pinned down in a fire fight in the middle east and got shot for his time there. He didn't really want to talk about it. I can't blame him. He kept calling me Sean Connery.

The night was getting on and the day had taken its toll so we decided to head back to our room just in the nick of time as the band had just began to play "I Will Survive". I hate that song. Georgia delighted in signing along to torment me. I only feared that ABBA would be playing in the discovator. Nope, just a drunken home girl. Good night New York!

Day 5: Going home.
We sleep late. Entirely understandable. We sort out what we are bringing back. Georgia is well over her allowable free duty limit. I take some of her items and she carries the 10 cigars that put me over my exemption. I also pack one of her shirts in my bag. It was a nice shirt. I liked it. She took it back.

There's only one thing left to do and that is my request. A trip to the Carnegie Deli. An iconic Jewish deli. It is raining again. On the way there Georgia buys one more gift.

The Carnegie serves wonderful coffee. Breakfast starts with Mozza ball soup. Why not? I order hot pastrami and Georgia

65

gets corned beef. Our server is Asian. I don't think she's Jewish. She drops off our sandwiches which require a forklift to deliver. I can no longer see Georgia across the table. Just rye bread and steaming pastrami. I will later regret having pastrami for breakfast. Of course a breakfast of this nature requires a gargantuan piece of New York cheese cake to finish off. We waddle home toting our leftovers. They don't make it. We already have a pile of takeout boxes in our room from other meals we couldn't finish but felt too guilty to leave on the plate. They also do not survive.

We get back to our room, finish packing then check out and wait. You always have to wait on your way home. Our journey back will take close to 12 hours. The flight is only about 5.

We are the first to be picked up by our shared shuttle. This means that we spend the next hour and a half meandering around Manhattan picking up other travelers. It is still raining and the shuttle is getting stuffy. The traffic is typical and Georgia wants to puke. I break one of the three ornaments I bought. Next time I will arrange a limo.

We arrive at Newark airport and find that we are at the wrong terminal. Fortunately they have a train that transports you from one terminal to the next. We attempt to get our boarding pass from the kiosk but it won't issue Georgia's. Her name is misspelled. This is only normal for her. A misspelled name has plagued her all her life. Sometimes at her own doing. We get things sorted out, get x-rayed and wait some more.

The flight home was thankfully uneventful other than the circular flight path out of Newark. Apparently there are a minimum number of turns that a plane must take when arriving at or leaving. We land in Vancouver where it is warm and the banana palms are in blossom only to discover that Air Canada has short changed YVR and they have been forced to park their planes as far away from customs as possible. The walk to the financial district was shorter.

We get through customs then wait for our bags. We are tired of waiting. I have become a bit cranky. Unusual for me. But we manage to retrieve our bags and meet her boyfriend outside. We sort out our things, hug and say goodnight. We have done New York.

HAPPY BIRTHDAY GEORGIA!

Dam Nation

There are a number of things in this world that frighten me; global warming, cockroaches, rats, psychos with guns, my mother-in-law. My wife's meatloaf can be a bit scary too. There are more but lists of that sort make me feel uncomfortable. There are pressing issues and abuses that we all should be very concerned about but I feel compelled to worn the world of what I consider to be a most disturbing trend that could spell certain doom for the human race. One that came to my attention many years ago and continues to grow in prevalence, relevance and outright dominance. Something so ghastly and premeditated I wonder that only I seem to have connected the dots and made the connections that can bring this conspiracy to light. I speak of a concerted effort by a specific species to rise up and take control of the planet. I speak of the BEAVER.

Yes, the beaver. Not El Qaida or the Taliban or apes or super volcanos or see through yoga pants but the beaver. That nasty, long toothed, flat tailed, tree chomping furry little beast. We should all begin preparing for the apocalypse that this creature has planned for us. Be afraid, be very afraid.

I first noticed their intent many years ago in the interior of British Columbia. My wife and I had gone to my in-laws cabin on Canim Lake for a vacation. As I was want to do, I arose early one morning and went fishing. It was a beautiful morning. Something out of a magazine like National Geographic or American Sportsman. The sun was just climbing out of the trees sending shafts of light piercing through a low mist that hung over the still water. I had forgone the use of the outboard motor and chosen to row as I felt anything else would be a sacrilege. I had made my way into a small cove and was so overcome with the moment that I lit a joint. Why not?

After achieving a reasonable buzz, I took some time to wallow in nature's awe. Weed will do that to you. This was truly amazing. I began to ready my fishing gear to do a little spin casting in hopes of catching a rogue trout or wandering bass or just snag a rotten stump when I noticed a small piece of wood floating in the water. It was an odd shaped piece of wood appearing to be somewhat similar to the head of a large rodent and it had eyes. This was interesting, a bit of floating debris that had eyes and they were staring at me.

Having grown up during the sixties and seventies, I am familiar with and full well understand the effects of marijuana. Paranoia and the munchies are not new to me. I was most certainly stoned but this log was staring at me. Malevolent eyes glaring across the water in my direction.

I put down my fishing rod very slowly and tried to discern exactly what this log's intentions were when it moved ever so slightly, rippling the water around it. OK, it's not a log but what is it?

A sense of foreboding came over me. A log should not have eyes and it should not move of its own volition. Something was wrong with this picture. Then it moved again. A bit more violently causing a few wakes to spread across the cove. It definitely had my attention. I looked about and noticed a large pile of debris near the shoreline and quickly deduced that It must be a beaver lodge and ergo the log was not a log but a beaver. I relaxed a bit. Just a beaver.

Then there was a splash. A very loud splash. It had slapped its tail on the water. I knew this was a display meant to frighten off intruders and it had worked. It had scared the shit out of me. Obviously the beaver was pissed. I had invaded its territory and it was letting me know that I was not welcome. Fine, I've been lots of places that I wasn't welcome. Screw you beaver.

There was another splash. This time there was an intensity that said "I mean business". I looked at the beaver and its beady little eyes were locked on me. I felt the chill of fear begin to creep up my spine. This was no ordinary beaver.

It began to swim towards my boat. Its teeth were bared and its tail slapped viciously at the water. It was a torpedo bent on destroying my vessel like a kamikaze pilot at Pearl Harbor. In spite of the fact that I was in an aluminum boat and had nothing to fear, I raised one of my oars to strike at it should it come to battle. It was then that I realized that the oar was made of wood and would be useless in a battle with a beaver. I would simply be feeding it instead of defending myself. With a final slap of its tail it slipped beneath the surface of the water. I was certain it was preparing for its assault and my impending doom.

There are two categorized responses to conflict in the animal world, fight or flight. I chose flight. This was one angry beaver and I didn't care if I was in an aluminum boat, I was under imminent attack from a beaver that was sure to kill me so I fired up the 9 horse power Evinrude and got the hell out of there before the furry torpedo struck. Back at the cabin I recanted the story to my wife who shrugged it off saying "You're stoned". End of flashback.

That episode haunted me for many years. I told the tale to my friends who laughed and shrugged it off but I knew this was an omen, a warning of darker things to come. I began to do some research and discovered that beavers are second only to humans in their ability to manipulate and change their environment. Think about that for a moment. Second only to humans at manipulating their environment. What are they up to? During the last ice age in North America there was a beaver that grew to more than 2.4 meters (8 feet to the metrically challenged) in length and weighed in at 60 to 100 kg (130 to 220 lbs.). Pretty much the size of a black bear. Its teeth were 15 cm (6 inches) in length. It was the largest rodent of its time. What if they had suddenly started to devolve?

There is at least one (and could be more) First Nations tales describing a giant man eating beaver that was clubbed to death by a benevolent spirit. Beavers have been slaughtered for their fur, for their glands used as medicine and perfume (apparently they have an FDA approved natural sweetener in their anal sacs) and because their harvesting of trees and flooding of waterways may interfere with other land uses. They might not be too happy about this and could be looking for some kind of revenge. I know I'd be a bit pissed if someone turned one of my family members into a hat.

Beavers are a reasoning animal and reportedly like to play practical jokes. I don't think the one that came after me was joking. They are excellent structural engineers. They are always "busy". Why? What are they up to?

I began to scour newspapers and then the internet (after dial-up modems went the way of the giant beaver) for stories and signs of beaver activity. News items began to crop up from around the world:

> - *Two sisters were seriously injured after a violent beaver attacked them at Lake Anna in Spotsylvania County, Va. They were swimming with family when they felt something scratching beneath them.*

Moments later, the 65-pound animal attacked and bit both of their legs.

- A 5-year-old boy was attacked by a beaver in Durant at the family's home in a new apartment complex in a heavily wooded area with a stream nearby.

- Angry beavers managed to successfully scare off locals taking over a bathing area in Lindesberg in central Sweden.

- A beaver that attacked a Boy Scout leader swimming in the Delaware River was killed after Scouts in the troop pelted it with rocks. 51-year-old Normand Brousseau, of Pine Plains, N.Y., was swimming in eastern Pennsylvania on Aug. 2 when a beaver swam through his legs and bit him in the chest. After initially throwing the animal from his body, it returned to continue the attack, biting Brousseau in the leg, buttocks, arm, hand and torso before he managed to grab it and hold its jaw closed. Brousseau threw the beaver ashore while Scouts helped him out of the water. After being momentarily stunned, the beaver began attacking a pool noodle.

- Wake County officials urged people to take caution around wildlife, after a beaver attacked two people at Falls Lake. The beaver approached them biting one swimmer and hitting the other with its tail, causing lacerations.

- According to the CBC, a beaver (Canada's national symbol) grabbed and bit a man that had run into it with his car.

- Vancouver's Olympic Village had a new resident beaver that was getting quite a bit of attention napping among the reeds in the sunshine. It was well photographed, popping up on a local blog and YouTube.

- Check out this video:
http://www.youtube.com/watch?v=WyZP6m69y5A

- A mad beaver was blamed for delaying traffic in Miramichi, N.B. A cab driver told the website that he later spotted a beaver chasing a man up his driveway on King George Highway. He had earlier seen a beaver on Pleasant Drive and assumed it was the same one. He hopped out of his car to snap a few photos but the beaver took an aggressive stance, slapping its tail on the ground and chased him back into his vehicle.

- An Edmonton woman warned other pet owners after her dog was attacked by beavers in the North Saskatchewan River. The dog sustained three gashes to his armpit (leg pit?) and stomach while retrieving a stick in an off-leash park near Whitemud Creek.

- A beaver bit a dog at Anchorage's University Lake dog park. The rodent chomped the dog five times on the rump.

- A Belarussian fisherman was bitten to death by a beaver after he'd tried to get a photo of the sharp-toothed critter. The animal's bite had severed a main artery and the man bled to death.

A pattern was beginning to form. These incidents could not be coincidental. Beavers were no longer cute little tree eating rodents that flooded valuable land, they were terrorists seeking revenge for years of abuses. They were assault troops causing mayhem and death. This was only the beginning, I was sure. It would only be a matter of time before rivers like the Mississippi, Amazon, Nile, Congo and Yangtze were blocked by massive beaver dams causing wide spread flooding and apocalyptic damage. I'm certain the beavers have factored in global warming to maximize the destruction. They may even be contributing in their own way. We don't know much about the Elks or Eagles or Masons so who knows what goes on in a Beaver Lodge? Michael Moore or Al Gore need to make a documentary about this!

They are plotting our demise, I swear it. Somewhere there is a beaver lodge laboratory where they are developing teeth that can bite through titanium alloy, carbon fiber and my wife's meatloaf.

Beware the beaver!

The Golf Trip

or

Flogging a Dead Course

One evening at my club (please do not conjure up visions of stuffy old goats sitting around in leather arm chairs telling war stories, it's really not like that, more of a tree fort kind of club), a few of my friends and fellow cigar aficionados collectively agreed that an excursion of the golfing variety was required in the near future. We discussed the "we shoulds" and the "we coulds" and promptly sent out invitations to prospective participants. A small committee, those that happened to be there at the time, decided on the duration and direction of our journey and which courses would provide the greatest amount of frustration and eventual comedy. As was explained to me "golf is a great game, you'll hate it."

Having settled on the primary itinerary, we would be travelling south into the wilds of the Pacific Northwest United States playing some challenging tracts of dubious reputation and difficulty. We then proceeded to discuss logistics. As we would be crossing the border the group was instantly divided into those with Nexus cards (a trusted traveler designation) and those without or in other words, those who could lie with a straight face ("no I never inhaled") and those with a mitigating police record.

Providing even greater confusion, one member was only coming down for the first day while another would be arriving later in the evening. Then there was the issue of who would allow cigar consumption in their vehicle and who wouldn't. This would be a trip that was longer than an hour and would obviously require at least one cigar to be smoked while travelling. I know that my own car won't even start without a cigar. A rare option provided by the dealership.

There would be seven of us travelling from points scattered about the Greater Vancouver area converging just across the border at our first test of all those anger management courses and antidepressants. It would appear that the minimum number of vehicles required to transport seven golfers is five. In an act of total self-deprecation, I volunteered to mount my Thule (a car top storage device) on the roof of my Volvo so that I could carry more than 2 sets of clubs with accompanying luggage. Thules have a certain cache amongst the soccer mom set but to me they are nothing more than a dorky appendage that clearly states "I have too much stuff and not enough car". When mounted on a Volvo a Thule can drive one's "cool" status well below subterranean in spite of the fact that they replaced the word "Thule" with "Volvo" in an attempt to create a designer feel to the black wart of increased fuel consumption attached to the roof. Mine had even more unique snob appeal in that it was not a "Volvo" Thule but rather a "Vol o" Thule. It seems that some up and coming rap star needed a "V" to hang on a chain about their neck. Fortunately, the Thule option was not required. We would assault the border in five separate vehicles, two with nexus, one returning later that day, one crossing in the evening all in some vain attempt to confuse U. S. border agents as to our true intent of terrorizing unsuspecting golfers, damaging properties foolishly built much too close to a golf course and removing large portions of American soil from its resting place.

We would consolidate to three vehicles once the Nexus elite had crossed the border in advance of the common citizen that had spent the requisite amount of time in border purgatory waiting to be grilled by an imposing, well-armed American border agent. "Would we be leaving anything behind?" Yes, several dozen golf balls and a much damaged ego.

Next on the agenda was a discussion on lodging. We would be staying in the Tacoma area which quickly ruled out the likes of a Four Seasons, Sofitel, Trump or Shangri-La chain leaving Holliday Inn and Best Western topping the list followed by Motel 6 and Super 8. Luxury was not an option but a smoking room was. A quick search on Google revealed a few establishments that allowed smoking in their rooms and on their premises. This is a very alluring consideration to a group of cigar smoking golfers. We opted for the Emerald Queen Casino and Hotel just off the I-5. We could smoke anywhere there. This was a luxury.

The itinerary was complete. Destinations, transport and lodging were in place. Other sundry details would be up to the individual participants and their respective therapists. All that was left to do was await the arrival of the appointed date. That and ordering cigars to be delivered to the home of a covert club member that lived below the 49th parallel, visits to medical practitioners to determine that we all were of sound enough health (mentally and physically) to accomplish such a taxing endeavor, stocking up on cheap golf balls and preparing lists of plausible excuses as to why a certain shot was struck in such a manner that the ball was never to be found in the encompassing time zone.

For myself, I spent a great deal of time planning my wardrobe. Golf is very much a fashion sport. One to be either mocked with a mismatched pair of sagging old cargo shorts and a faux designer polo shirt made from some form of synthetic fabric manufactured in a south east Asian country using a plethora of banned toxic substances and child labor or sporting color coordinated, logo infested designer outfits endorsed by any one of a number of PGA professionals guaranteed to make you look good while you topped a ball into the pond some twenty feet or so down the fairway. I chose three outfits patterned on the dress of a few favorite players; Phil Mickelson, Gary Player and Ernie Ells. The fourth outfit was put together from whatever clothes I had left that didn't require laundering and wouldn't down grade my fashion sense grade average. In packing for this trip I would adhere to my tried and true stratagem; when the closet and drawers are empty, I have enough clothes. Should we be invited to a black tie event or a showing of The Rocky Horror Picture Show, I would be prepared.

Time passed with great anticipation and enthusiastic discussion of the upcoming foray. This would be an epic journey the likes of which had not been seen since Marco Polo had opened trade routes to the Orient, Columbus had discovered the Americas, Neil Armstrong set foot on the moon or when my youngest daughter finally found Waldo. Soon the United States of America would be invaded by a merry troop of cigar smoking, club swinging Canadians bound on finding par, if not on the golf course then at least with our currency. Birdies were pretty much out of the question and whereas the Eagle is the national symbol of the U.S. we decided on calling any score less than a birdie a "beaver" thus substituting our own national symbol yet making it no more attainable. Besides, saying "I got a beaver" at our respective ages could be considered a major accomplishment, a dream fulfilled or an outright lie, any of which would be considered acceptable (I should mention to the uninitiated that beaver is a Canadian colloquial slang term for female genitals). The lie being preferable as most golf matches are fueled by bullshit.

The day of our leaving arrived and I felt more than adequately prepared having filled my vehicle with several pieces of luggage, my clubs, 3 pairs of golf shoes, snacks, cigars, a mason jar (for cigar butts and ashes) and a mound of items that I had remembered at the last minute (they were stored in my seasonal chest and thus did not see them when I was emptying my drawers and closet). If my travelling companion had more than simply his clubs, shoes and a small overnight case then he would have to be strapped to the hood like a recently slaughtered deer or (heaven forbid) I would have to mount the Thule in order to accommodate his belongings. I had also printed out several maps and emails that would guide us to our destinations and ensure that we would not get lost in Washington State and end up listening to some foreboding banjo music.

This proved to be a fruitless exercise as I had presumed that my companion (an architect) would be able to read and understand a map as I was sure he had dealt with much more complex documents such as blue prints, design concepts and the likes but as it turned out I was woefully wrong. While he deftly managed to identify the documents as maps, determining such things as north, street names, freeway exits and dead end roads seemed to be beyond his ken. We did manage to find a small farmers market where we purchased some free range eggs that could come in handy should we spy one of our compatriot's cars and feel the need to hurl yoke filled projectiles in a juvenile attempt at humorous vandalism. We also discovered that it was possible to drive beyond the map making the return to noted landmarks that much more difficult. This was accomplished miles past the turn off to the first course which we had both duly noted as being the wrong road in spite of it clearly being designated by a sign bearing the name of the course we were to play. Being adult males, stopping and asking someone for directions could not be considered as a viable alternative.

We wandered and backtracked enough to a point where, by sheer coincidence, my companion finally declared "here it is turn left". As we passed the sign proclaiming the name of the course I informed him that this was where we were to play three days hence. "Yes, but I found it" he joyfully stated reveling in his accomplishment. This was my own fault for I had not provided a daily chronological itinerary. We agreed to return to the initial sign and turn off that we had dismissed which (after only a few minutes of travel) took us to the course we were to play that day.

We met with our fellow playing companions who had no problems finding the course, had some lunch and proceeded to waste good shots and ingrain bad habits on the driving range. Then we golfed.

Later we convened at our friend's home beside the course that we had already visited to pick up the cigars that had been delivered there and leave one car behind in an attempt not to resemble an invading convoy as we headed further south into America. We had no problem finding it but there was a gate that barred our way into his subdivision. Thusly the name "Gated Community." This posed a problem as perhaps the only thing that I had not printed out for this journey was the email with the code to open the gate. It also had his phone number on it which seemed to be the only place it was recorded. Fortunately, technology came to our rescue for as we all know, if you send out enough text messages, something will happen. It did.

An hour or so later and we were on our way to Tacoma and the Emerald Queen Casino and Hotel which sat directly beside the I-5 and had a sign which was visible from the International Space Station thereby eliminating the need for my travelling companion to further degrade his cartographic skills, but first we had to stop for dinner.

The Fairhaven district of Bellingham is a resurrected port town which for some time was the haunt of many students from the nearby university. It used to be cool with small bars that attracted underground and alternative musicians and cheap restaurants that students could afford to eat at but it has now become trendy and a bit more upscale. This always seems to happen to student hangouts that start out as quasi bohemian/academic subculture villages that get discovered by the local tourist bureau. We liked it.

Our dinner took forever to get to our table because the place was full of tourists and undergrads with wealthy parents. A local cigar shop was the benefactor of the slow service. We ate and continued on arriving at the Emerald Queen at close to 10:00 at night. It had only taken 14 hours to drive from Vancouver to Tacoma (a 2 ½ hour drive) and play a round of golf. Pretty good time I'd say.

Finding the Emerald Queen was quite easy (turn right at the Poodle Dog Restaurant with retro American cuisine) but locating an entrance to the hotel and lobby was something completely different. There were several different turnoffs that lead to "do not enter" signs hung on the exterior of the parkade. We knew that you could get in because we saw cars in the parkade and assumed that they had been driven in as opposed to being placed there during construction to attract the wary gambler like decoys on a lake. After circumnavigating the hotel and parking lots several times we settled on what appeared to be the most likely driveway and as luck would have it, found valet parking and an entrance to the casino that did not indicate there was a hotel inside at all. There were a lot of armed security guys, a police car and what seemed to be several vagrants milling about. One vagrant had a suitcase so we assumed this must be how we get in to the hotel. Our suspicions were confirmed by an armed valet attendant. I opted to park my own car.

To get to the lobby of the hotel you must pass through the casino. Not an unusual scenario for any hotel/casino complex but passing through the Emerald Queen Casino was like walking through a Walmart with slot machines. Apparently when the customers finished purchasing their "rolled back" goods and said goodbye to the greeter they all came over to the Emerald Queen to spend the money they saved. I don't think I need to go into any descriptive detail here, just Google "as seen at Walmart" and you'll get the idea.

They had only slot machines at this location by the way, the other games were in a building further down and across the I-5 and accessible by a shuttle that ran every half hour. Maybe that's where the Target customers went. Shoppers from Fred Meyer are more bingo players than anything else.

Arriving in the lobby we greet the other member of our crew who had come down on his own missing the adventure of getting lost in Washington State. I should point out that he is probably 20 years junior to the youngest of the rest of us. There will be more to this point later. He informed us that he had already checked in and had been informed that "smoking" meant cigarettes only. No smoking cigars anywhere in or around the hotel. But I had a smoking room and no intention of asking if I could smoke cigars in it. What I didn't know wouldn't hurt them. Besides, I find it more spiritual to ask forgiveness instead of permission.

I strode up to the check in desk and the clerk with the 9mm Glock strapped to her hip asked for my name and all the other bits and pieces of cards and IDs needed to get a room. I was then required to agree to some incredibly lengthy document written in American Legalese which I did not read because, well who does? I could be selling my wife and family into servitude for all I knew. I agreed, because we all do. They make these things long on purpose because no one wants to lose 3 to 4 hours of their lives reading it let alone taking the post graduate courses required to understand it.

I gathered up my armada of luggage and headed up the elevator to my room. As I walked down the hall I could smell the pungent aroma of weed being burnt and I don't mean dandelions. Someone was smoking pot. I couldn't smoke cigars but someone was smoking pot and it was still a month before it would be legal in Washington State. There was irony here but I just couldn't quite put my finger on it.

The next morning we met for breakfast. This is not an unusual occurrence for anyone but I mention it as an opportunity to point out one of the basic differences between the sexes. The previous day, lunch was paid for by one person and dinner by another. Everyone else said thank you with no quibbling about the bill. The breakfast this morning was paid for by a third individual, again no quibbling. Subsequent meals would be dealt with in the same manner until everyone had paid for a meal. This is how a group of men deal with a bill. If someone offers to pay, say thank you and buy the next time. Women, on the other hand will spend an inordinate amount of time with each and every bill determining who had what, how much they owed and what the tip should be. It can involve pen and paper, a calculator or a main frame server at Microsoft. This discussion can last as long as it took to eat and lead to social disaster. Who cares who had the Chardonnay, say thank you and buy the next time.

After breakfast, all but the youngest of us took our anti-inflammatories, muscle relaxants and pain medications and went off to play golf. This required a drive of some 30 minutes or so to get to the course. My companion dutifully picked up the maps I had printed out prepared to guide us to our next destination. I was lighting a cigar at the time and felt the compelling urge to set fire to them and save us the aggravation of wandering about the Olympic Peninsula like Moses and his cohorts in the dessert. I opted to suggest that we merely follow the other vehicle so my companion could avoid any shame and derision should we get lost again. It also left us clear of blame should the others get disoriented instead. He agreed after seeing me reach for the fish bashing club I keep in the backseat in case I should come across a bass or tarpon swimming across the road. You never know.

Amazingly, we found the course without complication and spent the day waffling between mediocrity and atrocity with the odd moment of brilliance thrown in just to tantalize the golf senses into thinking there was a chance of making it on the senior's tour. Any golfer's worst round can be redeemed by one single glorious drive that whistles off the tee, rising as it sails down the fairway, drawing slightly into the center and rolling briskly forward to position "A" for attacking the green. This euphoria, however, is quickly destroyed when the next shot is shanked into a swimming pool of one of the houses built alongside the course.

This is something I have never understood. Why would anyone build a house on the fairway of a golf course? Insurance companies must salivate at the thought of rising premiums with every foundation that is poured. Local glaziers dance in jubilation as suburbs and links are mixed. Lawyers bankroll their next Porsches creating documents that absolve the course of any responsibility should an errant shot cause property damage or strike down a resident pruning the roses while puting the onus squarely on the shoulders of the golfer that hit the offending ball then making even more money defending said golfer in the resulting law suit.

Has no one ever seen the game of golf played? Advanced amateurs and skilled professionals alike and along with the rankest of beginners will hit shots that seem to take on a whole different understanding of quantum physics. The trajectory and flight of any given shot is not and cannot necessarily be contained within the confines of any fairway, rough or out of bounds stake no matter how much encouragement is given for the ball to "come back". It's like building a house on the flight path of an existing airport then complaining about the noise expecting it to stop.

I must confess that during this particular round I myself managed to lob no less than a half dozen balls onto the roofs of nearby homes much like an artillery battery shelling an enemy enclave. I am sure there are at least one or two skylights that suffered the wrath of my bombardment. But that's golf.

The day ended with a most enjoyable visit to "Smokey Joes", a cigar come sports bar located above a slot machine bingo hall full of Fred Meyers customers. Drinks were ordered with dinner so separate cheques were requested lest we be forced to give in to our feminine side when it was time to pay up. No need to say thank you.

The next morning started early as the World Cup was on and England was playing in the afternoon. One of our members was of obvious English decent (or at least the only one willing to admit it). This lead to much grumbling and groaning at the breakfast table. A round of tea was ordered as that seemed an appropriate beverage to celebrate the soon to be departed English national teams experience in the World Cup. What is the difference between the English soccer team and a tea bag? The tea bag stays in the cup longer.

This was the third day in a row for golf which would require a great deal more medication than first two. Stretching helps but a good shot of methocarbomal goes a lot further. One of our group did have some prescription pain medication which he would not share with the rest of us in spite of all the begging and pleading. Bastard!

Having solved the cartographic issue we found ourselves in due time on the first tee of this day's source of frustration. The smell of Voltarin and Rub A535 wafted across the tee box mixed with the pungent aroma of some strange Asian concoction guaranteed to loosen up the stiffest of muscles and improve your sex life. There was always a place that was sore that you couldn't quite reach with the medicated ointment but soliciting help from one of the others was out of the question. Men (heterosexual) do not rub things on other men (heterosexual or otherwise).

The stillness of the morning was broken by the sound of what could have been a large bowl of Rice Crispies just after the milk was poured on as each of us in turn bent to tee up a ball or pick up an Advil that had been dropped or strap on a knee brace. The "snap" and "crackle" were not of much concern but any "pop" was met with a round of "what was that?" The reply being some part of the anatomy that was not supposed to "pop".

There was another sound that became quite common. It was also cereal related not by simile, but reality as oatmeal and granola and flax and other whole grains have crept into our high cholesterol vocabulary and diet. Grasses and grains, as any cow or other herbivore will attest, cause gas. Gas causes flatulence and that causes noise.

I must admit with some shame and remorse that when it comes to farts, it seems men have not grown much beyond being ten year old boys. There is nothing as funny as a well-timed fart. Like in the middle of a backswing or a birdie putt or just before you get off a crowded elevator. Needless to say, there were plenty of laughs and several missed putts.

There was also an exploding golf ball and three pale and aging moons hung on the 17th green that lead to 2 lost balls. Three bare asses is one thing but the wrinkly dimpled chins dangling underneath must have been quite off putting. That kind of thing can never be unseen and can lead to nightmares and psychological trauma.

And of course there was pissing in the woods. This is a male tradition. A need it would seem. Men would prefer to urinate anywhere but in the facilities provided on a course. I witnessed one man peeing on the outside wall of an outhouse rather than step inside. Watching one of my fellow golfers standing in the weeds in relief, I was tempted to call his name and get him to turn around as I had noticed a great deal of tall growing poison ivy in the vicinity. Now that would have been much more funny than a well-timed fart. Nothing like seeing a grown man clutching and scratching at his dangling bits after dragging them across a poison ivy frond.

We finished in time to return to Smokey Joes and witness England lose their first match then stayed for several more hours enjoying beverages, cigars and dinner with separate bills none of which totaled more than thirty dollars. This was a phenomenal establishment in spite of the "bingo" calls from downstairs and we all declared how great it was get up early and golf.

The next day was our last and required a return north to Bellingham. No need for maps or follow the leader as the destination had already been found the first day. What was most interesting as we all prepared medically for the day was that our youngest cohort was complaining of the same aches and pains as the rest of us. Maybe all the pissing and moaning had finally gotten to him. Perhaps he was allergic to the smell of analgesic ointments. Could he have pissed on the poison ivy? Whatever the reason, we had managed to drag him down to our level! We celebrated with a round of Ibuprofen, Tylenol and a Tiger Balm rub down.

The last course was a bit of a challenge for all of us except the one who was a member. It seemed that a certain amount of local knowledge was a necessity in navigating this tortuous tract. My group started first with this member's group following. They had the advantage of being informed of the pitfalls that lay ahead on certain holes. We, on the other hand were treated to the phrase, "you shouldn't have hit it there" on too many occasions as our followers arrived on the tee box just after we had hit. We decided to play "hit 'til you like it" to compensate for the tardy directions. This lead to a great deal of lost balls but as long as you didn't like the shot, it didn't count. We scored well from that point on.

The day and the round concluded with the last man buying a late lunch for us all. We thanked him. A dinner reservation had been made for later on but we all begged off with excuses of having to get home to the wife or children or some other pressing engagement. The truth be known, I believe several chiropractic and acupuncture appointments had been made to be followed by a lengthy stay in a hot tub and a hyperbaric chamber. No pain, no game.

We parted company and headed back across the border, trunks full of duty free goods, bags devoid of golf balls and egos damaged beyond repair. We had all declared the journey an overwhelming success and vowed to do it again in the fall when hip replacements and spinal fusions had healed.

Next time I plan to seek sponsorship from Roche, Johnston and Johnston or Pfizer for the trip or at least buy some stock before we go.

On the Occasion of My First MI.

The month was January and the year was 2002. It had snowed and I was out in my front yard with my two daughters and one of their friends making a snow man. Things were rolling along just fine for a while until I noticed a twinge in my chest. Nothing alarming, just a bothersome little pain. Could be anything so, I ignored it.

I continued to struggle with a large ball of snow attempting to roll it up a small hill when my breath became a bit short, I began to sweat and the minor annoyance in my chest became something more. I stopped abruptly and excused myself and went around the corner of my house to squat a bit and compose myself. It was nothing, I was certain. I'm fine I assured myself.

A few minutes respite and I was feeling a bit better and returned to the front yard in time to heft the large ball of snow that was to become the torso onto its base. I bent and lifted then stopped. There was a sharp pain in my jaw, my left arm and my chest. I began sweating rather profusely and breathing was difficult. I remember thinking this might be a heart attack. I stopped my struggles and went to the front door and called my now ex-wife to come and take my place. I told her I wasn't feeling altogether well and needed a bit of a break. I would let her know how things were progressing. Could she please come out and keep an eye on the kids.

I wandered down the hall in pain and into my office where I sat down at my desk and pulled out a medical compendium. The internet was still a bit fledgling and unreliable as far as I was concerned and I trusted this particular collection of medical facts because after all it was published by Reader's Digest. You could trust them right? I also lit a cigarette (I was a smoker at the time) determined to at least have one last smoke before succumbing to cardiac arrest. Apparently this is not an unusual act but the irony and lunacy is quite profound. I calmly puffed away as I read the section on myocardial infarction and checked off the list of symptoms; chest pain – yes, puff, pain extending down the left arm and up into the jaw, puff, – yes, shortness of breath, puff – yes, perspiration, puff, – yes. Hmmm could be having a heart attack. What to do? The book said to lie down for five minutes and see if the pain subsides. If it doesn't, call a doctor or ambulance. So I put out my cigarette and lay down on my bed making note of the time on the clock.

An eternity later when the five minutes had elapsed, the symptoms had not gone away. I got up and took a couple aspirin as I recalled somewhere I had learned that this was the thing to do, then went to the window and called to my wife. "I think you should come in" I said "I might be having a heart attack. Don't tell the kids."

I lay down on the bed again and my wife came into the bedroom. We discussed briefly what to do and decided to call a doctor friend of ours who worked in the ER at our general hospital and lived very close. Unfortunately he was not home. We then decided to phone another doctor friend who also lived nearby. The issue here was, he is a gynecological oncologist. I was pretty sure my ovaries and uterus were fine but I figured if I was having an MI then I was fucked anyway and might as well call him. So we called and waited for his arrival.

While we waited it suddenly occurred to the both of us that if the situation was bad enough to resort to calling a gynecologist then maybe we should just call the ambulance as well. This turned out to be a very good idea. Our friend arrived and I became concerned that he would then examine my wife or put me in stirrups. He was very kind and asked a series of questions and took my pulse and all that and more or less confirmed that I was probably experiencing a heart attack and should call for an ambulance. He assured me there was nothing wrong with my cervix. No sooner had the words left his mouth when the sound of sirens filled the air and a fire truck accompanied by two ambulances pulled up in front of my house. It was then that my children suspected there was something wrong with Dad.

My bedroom was suddenly filled with three firemen, four paramedics, my wife and one gynecologist. A great deal of equipment was spread across the floor and the bed. Things were happening now. A defibrillator was prepared, although never required and an oxygen mask placed on my face just in time to answer the myriad of questions that I was assailed with and had to repeat to every ensuing individual that confronted my problem. There would turn out to be no less than 15 interrogators. The Spanish inquisition has nothing on our medical system. I later came to the realization that a voice recording unit should be given to every patient at the onset of treatment so that the questions that would be repeated endlessly by every attending professional or interested bystander could be answered at the push of a button instead of aggravating the patient, causing anxiety and worsening their predicament.

When it was determined that I was somewhat stable (my psychiatrist would disagree) the task of moving me to the ambulance began. Here is a note to all residential architects and designers, please bear in mind that there may come a time when a gurney needs to be brought into a structure and plan for that eventuality. As it turned out, our home was not designed to allow paramedical transport equipment into the bedroom. Could I walk to the driveway so they could put me on a stretcher? I'm having a fucking heart attack here, what do you think?

But that's what I did. Trailing hoses and wires and firemen and paramedics, my wife and one gynecologist. In the driveway they put me on a gurney and lifted me into the ambulance. I was taken to the hospital with sirens wailing and upon arrival given immediate attention. My wife had stayed home with the children while our doctor friend came with me in his Porsche. He's a surgeon, what did you expect? He was well-known and respected in the hospital which turned out to be a great asset when requiring attention in an emergency ward although the staff were a bit confused as to what part of me they should be examining.

The attending physician came into my curtained off cubicle to ask me all the same questions everyone else had already asked. I looked at his name tag and it read "Dr. Loser". It was not a confidence inspiring name. It occurred to me that should Nurse Goner show up I may not come out of this alive. I was examined, tests were done, blood was taken and I was sent off to the CCU where I was wired to a heart monitor, a vitals monitor, given an oxygen tube, some sedation and poked with two intravenous lines. All this time my friend was there with me. A few hours later, my wife showed up. Maybe one of the indicators that she would eventually become my ex. The sedation kicked in and I drifted off into a land full of killer snowmen being chased about by speculum wielding gynecologists. It seemed perfectly normal that every snowman had a heart beating where his genitalia should have been. The fact that snowmen have no genitalia, gender specific or not, did not occur to me. I also had no idea what the gynecologists intended should they have captured one.

The next day I was to be given an angiogram to see what had caused the MI and what the extent of the damage was. My gynecologist friend was doing his rounds early that day and came by my bed to see how I was doing. I should explain that he is a highly educated man with two degrees from much respected universities. He is tall and slender, fairly attractive and of wealthy German decent. He had had a very proper upbringing. He was also married with two children of his own. While we were talking, a male nurse came by, one that had been on duty when I was brought in the night before, he looked at me and then my friend and said "We could have brought you a cot so that you could have stayed with him all night". The implication was quite obvious. He thought we were lovers. I chuckled a bit to myself while my friend became quite flustered. This was beyond his comfort zone and to imply that he might be gay was too much for him to handle. He bid a quick goodbye and rushed off never to be seen at my bedside again. The nurse gave me a look of consolation.

A bit later, a different nurse, female this time, came by to prep me for the angiogram. A probe was to be inserted in the femoral artery of my right leg. This site is very close to some personal bits that I am quite attached to. The preparation was to shave the area where the incision was to be made. She lifted the covers and exposed my nether regions then reached for some shaving cream and a razor. Now any man can attest that there may not be a more frightening sight than a women with a razor hovering over your naked genitalia. This, I think, is what caused my heart to palpitate and bring on a secondary M.I. I explained to her what was happening and she abruptly put down her tools and ran out of the room. Odd reaction I thought. Perhaps she didn't wish to witness my expiration.

Minutes later she returned with a technician and an ECG machine. It would seem that they wanted to record the event as it happened. I wanted drugs to make it stop. Ten little patches were placed about my body and I waited in pain while the paper slowly crept out of the machine. At the appropriate time all ten leads were torn off in a single stroke causing a great deal of auxiliary pain. This must have been some form of new treatment that was meant to make one forget about the pain in one's chest by providing a whole different level of pain in several other areas. Something was injected into one of my intravenous tubes, nitro was squirted under my tongue and my crotch was brutally shaved. Whatever the injection contained made me forget not only my deep seated male fears of women and razors but also that I had genitalia at all.

I was subsequently wheeled off to a room full of other similarly drugged individuals awaiting the insertion of wires and cables into places they didn't belong. When my turn came up I was taken into a lab and laid on what I can only describe as a narrow plank. No, that would be much too complimentary, it felt more like a steel I beam used in the construction of skyscrapers. It had the same rigid level of give coupled with that embracing cold that only steel can provide. I think they left some rivets in it by the feel of things. Comfort was obviously neither a consideration nor necessity for the procedure.

Prior to beginning, I felt it was time to distract the good doctor from slicing into my femoral artery and possibly completing the damage intended by the razor wielding nurse in pre-op by asking some poignant questions and making a few vital pleas for more anesthetic to address the imminent pain and something to relieve the consciousness I was enduring. Surely the patient needed to be immobilized for this? Nope. They need the victim awake and aware, something I have tried to avoid since the late 60's.

"Would I feel anything?" I asked.

"Nothing at all, totally painless. Perhaps a little discomfort but that is all." Replied the intrepid swordsman threatening my inner thigh.

"Have you ever had one of these done to you?" A fair question I felt.

"No" he responded.

"THEN HOW THE HELL DO YOU KNOW WHAT IT FEELS LIKE" was my rather over enthusiastic retort. At which point I could feel a scalpel open a wound large enough for small pleasure craft navigation.

My cry of obvious agony was ignored with the comment "You didn't feel that" which caused a knee jerk reaction from myself, literally, as my other leg came in contact with the surgeon's ribs giving rise to an "oof" or some such other comic book exclamation.

"You didn't feel that" I said through a sarcastic grin. I was quickly treated to a shot of nerve numbing agent and the procedure proceeded.

Now in truth, one cannot actually feel the device being forced through your arteries like a rotor router through house plumbing but your one mind cannot help but imagine one of those animated maps from old timey movies that plot the flight of a hero's travels to Tibet or deepest darkest Africa. It's easy to conjure a plaque munching propeller leaving a red trail behind it as it wends its way up from your nether regions to the vicinity of your beating heart (a metaphor of some tribal death ritual awaiting our hero). Heavy sedation is a boon to this mental meandering.

What one can feel is the inflation of the small balloon like apparatus that they use to open up your clogged arteries. I find I am wondering why Draino or Liquid Plumber hasn't come up with some household solution to this problem. It's pretty much the same context as clearing a plugged toilet. Anyway, they managed to plow aside the offending plaque dams and insert several stents resembling Chinese finger traps into the non-functioning arteries that surround the "old ticker."

Problem dispensed of I was wheeled back to my cubical in the CCU for post-op care which consisted of literally clamping the leg with the severed artery to my bed with a "C" clamp the size of Rhode Island immobilizing not only the leg but the entire body of the patient for at least an hour allowing the artery to heal and avoid bleeding to death. I suppose this was a reasonable trade off but it provided no great deal of joy to consider it at that moment. Comfort and heart care are not synonymous. The only consolation to the tortuous leg clamp was a brief massage from a passing orderly following the procedure. I'm not sure if this was standard operating procedure or not as he left me his phone number and asked me to give him a call should I ever dump the doctor. I can only surmise that rumors of my friend's innocent appearance at my bedside had made the rounds. I chuckled at the irony of a gay gynecologist and considered it a brilliant name for a revival Broadway musical.

The remainder of my treatment and care in the hospital passed with relatively few incidents other than the appearance of my GP who not only embarrassed himself professionally but proceeded to make my children cry, lose me as a patient and receive a complaint to the medical practitioners board all in one brief 3 minute diatribe. He needs to "practice" medicine a bit more.

I returned home to absolutely no fanfare ("We didn't want to excite you"), a household purged of all tobacco products and accessories and a wilting snowman on the front lawn. Someone had jammed a wire into it from its lower extremities up into its thorax. The symbolism was not lost on me. There was also a bright red cardboard heart pinned to his chest. I smiled to myself thinking home is where the heart is.

On the Occasion of my Second MI.

As the saying goes, once is never enough. In this case, the saying is wrong.

I cannot remember the month but I'm pretty sure it was in the spring and the year was definitely 2005.

Our children had both gone out for the night to sleep over events with friends. At least that's what they told us and as it had been some time since my wife (now ex) and I had any time "alone" together we decided to throw caution to the wind and believe them. We went out for an enjoyable dinner of East Indian food at one of our favorite restaurants before returning home for movie night. Having a TV in our bedroom we opted to watch our movie there.

One thing led to another and not fearing any interruptions or the need to explain why mommy had suddenly become so interested in God, we were soon involved in vigorous and enjoyable sexual activities. After both of us had achieved what would be considered the ultimate goal and I in particular was catching my breath, I began to feel not quite right in a familiar sort of way. Short of breath, sweating, chest pain radiating up into the jaw and down the left arm. Not the usual signs of a pleasant encounter.

Having experienced these feelings before, I pretty much knew what was transpiring and dreaded the thought of having to give up sex this time around as the last heart attack lead to my quitting smoking. As it turned out my concerns about sex were a bit prophetic but it had nothing to do with my present situation.

I was sure that I was suffering at least angina pains if not another Myocardial Infarction. Several shots of Nitro did nothing to stop the pain (it had expired as it later turned out) so I asked my wife to call the paramedics while I put on some pajamas (I was damned if I was going to have my ass hanging out at the hospital) and laid down on the couch in the living room.

Last time, the ambulance folks could not get the stretcher into my bedroom and I was required to walk to my driveway in order to climb on the gurney and then be lifted into the ambulance. I didn't feel like walking this time and assumed they could get something into my living room that would transport me to the ambulance. I was mostly correct. The gurney was still a no go but they did manage to get a chair into my living room. A very square chair covered with a flannel blanket. It made me think of one of those very upright chairs you see in the front of a church. I was not interested in wearing the pointy hat that might come with it. Not to fear, no hat, but seat belts like you wouldn't believe. I was strapped in like an astronaut preparing for take-off. A bit of a Jewish wedding ride and I was out in the driveway where I still had to get out of it to get in the stretcher that would finally go in the ambulance. This will become a theme in my life.

In the ambulance on my way to the hospital I had my gender preference challenged by the male paramedic that provided me with a shot of morphine. Anyone that could make me feel that good deserved some consideration as a lifelong partner.

Fortunately, there was no Doctor Loser waiting for me at the emergency ward, not that I cared as I was quite stoned by the time I got there. I was quickly admitted and whisked off to a cubicle in the CCU where I received the same ministrations as I had on my previous visit and similar inattentiveness from my, as I have mentioned, ex-wife who did manage to show up at the hospital on the same day as my "event" showing incredible concern for my well-being and that of my beneficiaries. My gynecological friend did not come by preferring to avoid any gay innuendo.

Once the excitement had worn off and the crowds had departed I was introduced to the nurse who would become my personal angel and steal away my heart (figuratively). As I lay in bed that evening I found sleep eluded me, funny how a heart attack will get the old adrenaline pumping. I spoke with this vision in scrubs about my dilemma to which she held up one finger as if to pause my thoughts and said "I have just the thing" and quickly darted off in search of whatever that thing might be. She returned in but a trice with a syringe which she plunged into my intravenous line and said "Good Night!" I was swiftly overcome by unconsciousness and some very strange dreams.

The following morning I was awoken and prepared for my second angiogram. Fortunately I knew what to expect and when the nurse arrived with razor in hand and withdrew the blankets to expose my genitalia I suffered only mild embarrassment and avoided the palpitations of the previous visit. Then off to the catheter lab where the surgeon would inject my arteries with a warm dye that produced the strangest of sensations. Something between a mild orgasm and a good bed wetting coupled with a case of diarrhea. This was followed by a demonstration of intra-arterial balloon animal tying. I don't care what they say, when someone blows up a balloon in an artery of your heart you feel it. It is not a natural thing and your body wants to let you know about it.

Another stent was inserted, which could have been done in the first go around but they wanted to wait until the artery was well and truly plugged up before going in with an arterial plunger. What they had not anticipated was that an embolus had broken free of the blockage, much like a glacier calving icebergs, and lodged itself a little farther along the artery which was fortunate as if it had travelled to one of several other destinations I could have been either dead or a side serving of your favorite vegetable.

Be that as it may, I was fixed up and sent back to the CCU for clamping. My favorite nurse was fortunately on duty and was assigned to my bondage detail. I complained vociferously about the stress and strain that the procedure caused, pouting with great integrity. My personal saint once again raised her finger in the air and said "I have just the thing" and much like the previous instance, disappeared only to swiftly return with a syringe of clear liquid that was added to the cocktail being drip fed into the back of my left hand. After a moment I asked again about the clamping procedure to which she replied "Oh, we're done". Magic. Absolute magic. I was in love.

No matter the quality or ability of whoever does the angiogram procedure there is always a residual and lingering pain that accompanies it. I'm not sure why inflating a beach ball in an artery attached to your heart should cause any disruption or discomfort but it does. When my savior inquired as to my condition following the clamping ceremony I explained that I was experiencing some pain to which she replied..............wait for it............."I have just the thing".

Once more a magic syringe was conjured up and inserted in my intravenous line. "Say when" my glorious nightingale asked and began to press on the plunger. I felt a warm wave of relaxation come over me and the lights above my head began to change color and dance a bit. I held up a finger and she paused. Once all had settled to an ethereal paradise I waved her on and she squeezed yet more of whatever happy juice the needle contained into my system. The summer of love overwhelmed me and I spent the remainder of my day drifting through Elysium fields.

Once again my treatment was completed and I was released into my own recognizance. I returned home to less of a fanfare and more of a humdrum existence. My concerns regarding giving up sexual activity due to my heart attack were theoretically unfounded according to my cardiologist however my ex failed to haves that discussion with her. I have decided that in the future I shall wear my heart upon my sleeve for ease of access and should I suffer another MI I will immediately proceed to my driveway and lie down there.

On the Occasion of My Third M.I.

The following story is absolutely true and involves an act that I'm sure all men have participated in. It is said that there are two types of men. Those that masturbate and those that lie about it.

The third time is the charm they say. What do they know anyway?

Arguably this may have been my fourth heart attack but I have discounted the second one as it took place in the hospital and was clearly brought on by a female brandishing a razor having just exposed my genitalia. I consider that to be a normal reaction from any male in a similar situation.

The date was August 21st 2017 and the sight was my living room. A new living room as I was now divorced from my not so significant other of my previous M.I.s and now residing in a quiet suburb. I had managed to get beyond the complications of a divorce and began working on a "new" me. I was down 45 pounds (a little more than 20 kgs. for the metrically inclined) and trying to develop some "definition". I had also, fortunately, become involved with a special someone. Unfortunately, this involvement was long distance and therefore conducted mostly online.

As part of my renewal I had been walking and working out with some free weights as well as a few other exercises. This, of course, lead to some stiffness and sore muscles which should be expected. More on this later.

Now my girlfriend and I had been communicating for about 6 weeks and had become quite close. As can happen in these times and technologies we had discovered digital intimacy. As any other day I sat in my recliner enjoying a coffee in the morning when I received an incoming message on my phone. A forewarning of things to come. It was my friend, lover, partner, whatever, checking in. While we chatted I lifted some free weights hoping to develop my pecs enough to make them bounce at will. I knew this was irresistible to any female so I put in just a little more effort this morning. An action I would come to regret.

Now conversations can take many twists and turns. This one twisted and turned into something quite sexual. The result was predictable. I put down my dumbbell to free a hand for other pursuits. While I was working out the stiffness in my muscles there was another stiffness that was arising. I noticed tightness in my chest but put it down to a bit of over excursion and muscle strain caused by my quest for perfect pecs. Actually, I was simply trying to tighten up some of the excess skin that hung loosely in odd places after losing so much weight so quickly. Vanity thy name is flesh.

In spite of swapping the free weights for something a bit more aerobic, the tightness in my chest did not subside but being somewhat absorbed in more personal erotic pursuits at the urging of my girlfriend, I ignored it. We men can be a bit linear in our thinking at times.

The non-verbal conversation intensified becoming more explicit and graphic. I doubled my efforts increasing the tempo of my endeavors encouraged by divine and lustful images provided in erotic text form. My partner was impassioned and inspired by my responses of written expressions of pleasure and indulged her own fantasies. Things were becoming heated.

My living room has a large picture window through which I can be clearly seen from the street and I felt this was a bit more exposure than I was willing to accept. It had become time for a change of venue least my mail carrier discover me in a compromising situation and withhold delivery. I rose and moved to a more private location without losing a beat. The tightness in my chest had become a minor pain but as I was in the throes of self-indulgence, I ignored it. There were other more pressing concerns at hand.

I sat down in my office and placed the phone in such a position that I could keep up with the story line while continuing to take care of business. I must compliment my girlfriend on her skills as an erotic composer of fine literature. It certainly captured my attention and imagination spurring me on with some urgency. A little too much urgency as it turned out.

It soon became apparent that the pains in my chest were something more than simply muscle strain. Having experienced the symptoms of a heart attack in the past I was pretty sure I was now experiencing them again. This presented a dilemma. I was not only very close to completing the task in hand but a possible cardiac arrest as well. What to do?

In spite of facts and history, being male does have its drawbacks. We are driven by certain primal urges not the least of which is procreation or at least the act that results in perpetuating the human race. Of course procreation requires that the male must achieve orgasm in order to generate new life. This may be the single most important reason as to why it feels so damn good to do so (orgasm that is not necessarily to hang around and raise the offspring). Regardless of whether the act is one of procreation or simple self-gratification the drive to reach climax is quite compelling. This was the source of my dilemma.

My problem was further enhanced by the ongoing dialogue with my girlfriend who was herself very much enjoying the experience. Did I encourage her to stop so that I could perhaps stave off my impending death? Of course not. I said nothing (well I was a bit vocal but nothing I was saying had anything to do with halting the course of action).

I pressed on in greater haste hoping to finish off before I expired. I knew it was going to be a close race but I had every bit of confidence that I could cross the finish line alive with enough time to call the paramedics. If not, I would at least go out with something resembling a smile on my face having managed one last moment of orgasmic bliss. Sure it was not the most ideal ending but at that moment it felt like a pretty good alternative in spite of the intense pains in my chest and other classic symptoms associated with a heart attack.

As unbelievable fortune would have it, the narrative and my endeavors reached climax at the same time. Something almost unachievable under normal circumstances let alone when one is on the edge of death while sexting and masturbating (there I said it).

There are moments in life that can be described as intense. There are others that seem to transcend the reality of the moment, many of which occur during the act of having sex with another person. Seldom do they come about during solo gratification however when one is faced with coming and going at the same time it adds a whole new dimension to the moment, take my word for it. Without indulging in further description, I think you get the idea.

Release is an amazing thing, very fulfilling and a bit messy. When it also means that you can finally call 911 and hopefully live to tell this tale, it goes well beyond that. When the sensations subsided I informed my partner that I was experiencing some very familiar pains in my chest and that I was calling emergency services. So much for cuddling and cooing.

No matter how many times one says "Don't worry, I'm ok" it never helps. People will worry especially when those words are followed by "I'm going to the hospital". My girlfriend was obviously concerned and I tried to dispel those feelings while simultaneously calling emergency services, cleaning myself up (this was going to be difficult enough to explain to the paramedics the way it was without complicating things) and contacting my daughters.

I sat in my recliner, which is a mere ten feet from my front door, hoping that this time the gurney would be able to access my living room and I would not be required to get myself outside. This was not to be. I should have known and simply gone out and lay down on my driveway.

When I called 911 and asked for an ambulance they inquired as to what the issue was. I told them I was having a heart attack. The responder was skeptical and asked how I knew. "Because I've already had three of them and I know what it fucking feels like" was my reply. I was a bit testy. He asked about the circumstances that led up to my predicament and thus began my journey into excruciating embarrassment.

I knew the drill all too well. I was about to be questioned by no less than a dozen different individuals about the circumstances surrounding my heart attack. This was going to require some very imaginative use of the English language to explain without actually delving into the bare facts. I failed miserably. The situation did not allow the time for the creative thinking required to come up with a plausible yet false explanation. Of course, as karma would have it, the majority of the attendees turned out to be female. Perfect. I must applaud whoever filled out the hospital admitting report for their extreme discretion however I'm sure the truth spread as I heard a great deal of snickering during my stay in the CCU.

As I have hinted at, the gurney could not get into my house and I was required to walk out to it. I was strapped in and loaded into the ambulance. The two female critical care response members joined me and started hooking me up to all the necessary apparatus while asking me what had brought on the pain. They managed not to break out into outright laughter at my explanation but I'm sure I detected smirks and giggles. After a quick ECG the one informed me that I was indeed having a heart attack. "I fucking know that!" I explained, still a bit testy.

At that moment I saw a look pass between them as one began to apply the shiny foil pads to my body that are used for defibrillating machines. I became a little concerned and said so. "Just a precaution" I was told as the paramedics exchanged a rather knowing look while sizing me up for a body bag. I think they were lying.

The journey to the ER was surprisingly quick and uneventful other than my begging for morphine, avoiding the word "masturbating" and regretting my decision to be an atheist. I had also come to the opinion that my girlfriend had actually tried to kill me. I had no reason for this but in the state I was in anything was possible. We laughed about this later but she sounded a little less than genuine. A misunderstanding I'm sure.

The paramedics and hospital staff were all very professional and discrete. I survived (obviously) and lived on though became wary of any sexual activity as this marked the second time it had caused me to go to the hospital. Fortunately, I am male and those thoughts disappeared with the encouragement of my girlfriend, shortly after leaving the hospital and in spite of my cardiologist's warning not to indulge in sex for thirty days. I'm certain she's not trying to kill me, but even so, what a way to go.

8 Days in Havana

Friday, February 22, 2013

It is two days until I leave for Havana. I am a pilgrim going to Mecca preparing to circle the great cubic obelisk, one of the devout, prostrating myself with every step. I have been getting ready for days and find it difficult not to keep telling any and every one that I am going. Smug is my overcoat.

I approach the coming journey like a general anticipating battle. I have done my research, kept close track of the weather, surveyed the maps and made my plans for attack. I have grilled and questioned those that have gone before me. I anticipate reaching Nirvana, dwelling on Olympus or reveling in the halls of Valhalla. I am a brother of the leaf and I am going to the Cuban Cigar festival.

Saturday, February 23, 2013.

A single Sunday. That's all that remains between here and Havana. I have spent the day preparing to pack. Selecting and sorting clothing that will provide just the right mix of cool and attitude. Festivals require costumes and I have chosen mine carefully.

Then there are the bits and pieces, the necessities of life and travel. Meds and supplements, electronic devices and their accompanying chargers, sun glasses and sun block, books and pages of research, maps, itineraries and my passport, shit, my passport and my tickets. Then toothpaste, deodorant, razor and all that other crap that might be needed and inaccessible in a third world country which, as far as I'm concerned, is anywhere but Canada and the continental United States.

I need a steamer trunk.

Foolishly, I iron all my shirts and pants. Worse yet, I polish my sandals.

Sunday, February 24, 2013

Tomorrow. What more can I say?

Monday, February 25, 2013 – Underway

God awful early but who cares? I am going to the Cigar Festival in Havana. Just two short nonstop flights and I'm there. I had to arise with plenty of time for coffee and a cigar before heading off to the airport. It was going to be a long time until the next one.

My plane was delayed in Toronto due to a mechanical issue. I hate that. They always say it was a minor problem but you know that they were furiously applying duct tape to the landing gear. When we finally boarded I knew that if we did manage to get off the ground we would never get down in one piece. As we bounced and jostled our way over Florida, I could only hope that the super glue they applied to the wings would hold.

It did and we landed safely at Havana Airport where my herding instincts took me with the flow of the crowd to the customs and immigration area. It reminded me of the betting wickets at an old horse track. A short 45 minutes later I was formally admitted into Cuba where I was greeted by a large and loud Cuban gentleman holding a Rob Norton sign. His name was Conrado. He gave me a late night guided tour by Taxi ride through the suburbs of Havana to the drop off point where we then walked three blocks to my hotel because cars are not allowed in this part of old Havana. Quaint!

I am greeted at my hotel, the Conde de Villanueva, with a bottle of rum and a cigar, a reasonable beginning, but then I learned my first lesson in Cuba. Be patient. Nothing happens quickly. Service is not a well-developed concept here. I persevered and was rewarded with a room and several lessons on how to open the safe and retrieve the items I had locked inside.

The hotel is a bit tired or picturesque, depending on your outlook. It has a certain patina about it. The arm falls off my chair as does the paint on the walls. The ceilings are close to twenty feet high with cedar beams painted green. The bed is firm and single. It has all the charm I am seeking in old Havana. It is perfect. It has peacocks. Ornery old peacocks and a chicken and a cat. I will come to learn that chickens are not unusual. I will also learn to watch my step in any hotel lobby that has peacocks wandering around.

During my stay I will visit many of the 4 and 5 star hotels. The lobbies at least are grand and luxurious but could exist anywhere in the world. They are something and nothing special at the same time. The Conde de Villanueva could only exist in Old Havana and that is something special. One constant in all of them are Bonsai. Japanese plants scattered throughout the Havana urban landscape. An oddity I simply accept.

A quick change of clothes and I went down to the bar just off the courtyard. I stayed up a bit late smoking my second cigar of the day with a young blonde woman from Lithuania via London and Marcel, the bartender. She worked at a fashion house in London and Marcel (which also turns out to be the name of one of the peacocks) had consumed enough wine to be quite talkative and more open than he claimed he should have been. It was a very interesting conversation but more on that later. I will not see Marcel (the bartender) at the hotel for the rest of my stay. It was time for bed.

Tuesday, February 26, 2013 - It's Cuba

My first morning in Havana. I have awoken in a dream. I had set my alarm for 7 am and found I was entirely unoffended when it shouted at me. I did the morning thing and went down for breakfast and a cigar. This is when I met my tour partner Ioannis, a 38 year old plastic surgeon in residence from London. We ate and chatted until Conrado arrived and took us on a walking tour of old Havana.

As I said, there are no cars allowed in old Havana. There are no guns allowed as well. I feel safe everywhere but on the streets where cars are allowed. The cars are of course famous, renowned worldwide for their vintage and ability to continue to operate. Some are elegant and elaborate restorations and others are frightening in their dilapidation. In an ironic slap in the face to Russian American relations, American cars run on Russian Lada engines.

There are statues everywhere. Figures cast and carved litter the city depicting more heroes, saints, monarchy and political figures than I could possibly remember let alone name. There were two that do stick in my mind, however, a bust of Abraham Lincoln and another of John Lennon whose glasses go missing and reappear on a regular basis.

Cuba is in transition. At least physically. Politically is another story. It is a country built on dichotomy. Two currencies. Two standards of living. Two economies. Two faces. Some, like Conrado and Michael, the tour operator, believe it is a time of opportunity and growth. Marcel the bartender would disagree. There are many beggars on the streets but unlike our homeless they all have shelter and some sort of sustenance. A Cuban family receives only what they are given by the government but me as a tourist can have whatever I want. During times of shortages, the Cubans go without but the hotels do not. The harbor is being torn down and reconstructed to accommodate cruise ships and attract tourists. In spite of the embargo, Americans visit and talk of investing in Cuba. Canada established formal relations with Cuba in 1945 and along with Mexico, was one of the only two countries in the hemisphere to maintain uninterrupted diplomatic relations with Cuba following the Cuban Revolution in 1959. Fidel Castro was a pallbearer at Prime Minister Pierre Trudeau's funeral.

We come across a construction crew working on a trench rebuilding infrastructure underneath the cobblestones. I count 17 men, three of whom are engaged in actual physical labor while the others watch, confer, consult or sit on the curb and smoke. Old Havana is being renovated and rebuilt but I can't help but think they are simply creating another old world tourist trap. Old, very old buildings squat next to relatively new ones. Cobblestones are dug up and replaced. But underneath the reconstructing facade, there lies a Cuba that has suffered under embargo and dictatorship. There is a history here that will become another attraction like a Disney park. Is it worth it? Lust is fleeting and fickle. Love is enduring.

I don't know what to make of this. Old and grand Spanish architecture, too long neglected, is being brought back to life, but for what purpose? When do they build the first Starbucks or McDonalds?

The Cuban people are alive. There is music in the streets. They smile and greet me openly. The women are round and can be beautiful. Cubans it seems do not fit a mold. Some seem

Pilipino or African and others are purely Caucasian. There is no standard look that says "I am Cuban".

After the walkabout, we meet with Michael in the lounge of the Habanos store in our hotel and he tells us that some things have fallen through with our tour but others have materialized. "It's Cuba" he explains over a complimentary beverage and cigar. The cigars are wonderful and abundant. The store in my hotel will become my personal humidor.

We discuss possibilities, perhaps the Tropicana or the exhibition floor and come up with solutions that we can all live with, but you never know, things could change again. He provides envelopes with invitations to private events as consolation. It's a start. We have lunch at the Lamparilla, an outdoor café just around the corner from the hotel. The food is basic but good. The service is Cuban. The cost is 4.75 CUC ($5.00 Cdn). I have brought an insane amount of cash.

We part company with the assurance that Michael will meet us later and take us to the Parque Central Hotel where we can board a festival bus to the Opening night festivities at El Morro, the fortress across the bay.

A brief nap, a shower and change of clothing and it is time to leave. I have chosen to wear a fairly bright silk shirt with a tropical motif. This is the Caribbean and surely this would be the style. I would be alone, except for some women and the entertainers.

We gather at the appointed time and begin the short walk the Parque Central. Halfway there, Michael mentions tickets and I return to my room. Not to worry, you are never late in Cuba. Only fools are on time.

The route we take is on a street that is neither renovated nor even close to the process. The cobblestones are rough and uneven. The buildings, old, jaded and worn. This is not a pretty section of Old Havana. There is garbage on the street and a few old cars. This is not the Havana we were shown in the morning. That's good. I needed to see this.

At the Central we see no busses. We see no one waiting. No signs or officials to guide us. Several inquiries produce no information. The hotel staff are blissfully unaware that the cigar festival is even on. There will be no bus. It's Cuba.

Michael acquires a taxi and pays for our trip to the fortress. After crossing the bay through a tunnel we turn and come to the crest of a hill. There are cars and people milling about. There are lights and a couple of banners flanking two Spanish guards from the 18th century. We have a theme! But it's Cuba, so we wait. The crowd is eclectic. Cigar smoke wafts across the evening breeze. There is a sense of anticipation. We stand at the top of a sloping stone path that leads to the gates of the fort. It is treacherous enough in sensible footwear but the women wear heels in defiance.

Without fanfare at all, the gates open and two more costumed guards, replete with bayonetted muskets provide us entry. It is a long narrow hall that takes us to the grand entry and it is there that the spectacle begins.

Our hosts and their minions are all dressed from the period. The late 1700's. Mostly Spanish but some in native Cuban attire. There are women in red dresses, young men in white blouses and black pantaloons. We are handed a gift bag, cigars, a cutter and a lighter, this will become the standard for all events to come.

Down one more hall to the courtyard we are pressed and stand shoulder to back. The men are dressed in whatever but the women have come for a show. I am told the women of Cuba are the sexual aggressors. They strut and they preen and they flirt on the streets and complain if they don't catch an eye. Staring or ogling or making a comment is considered not only acceptable but expected by most women who will provide you with a dirty look if you don't provide them with a lascivious one.

The stage is set. The wait is short before a dark haired woman in a red dress steps on and begins the event. This is as much a conference as a festival so certain formalities must be addressed. After the introduction by the woman in red we hear from officials and presidents and other such dignitaries. And then it begins.

The band comes to the stage and fires up a driving Latin rhythm. Doors on the side of the courtyard are swung open revealing three hallways filled with a cornucopia of foods. Beverage stations open and literally swill rum, beer and wine into glasses to consume at will. There are a plethora of servers that tour the fortress in period costume. This is now a fiesta.

First to the food. We elbow and squirm our way through the crowds of diners and feast from the many tables and rooms filled with food. With brilliant luck we finish our gastronomic stroll at the massive cake that is our dessert. Then to the sprawling labyrinth that is the fortress.

It is a maze of stone walls, walkways and rooms. There are no less than seven different stations serving beverages that could satisfy any desire. There are stages and performers strewn about the grounds. The tower, which has now become a lighthouse, is lit with dancing images and changing graphics.

There are spotlights and search lights and lasers blaring color into the night. There are bagpipes. Yes bagpipes and you have not lived a full life until you have heard bagpipes play salsa. Here a string quartet, there a solo guitar, behind me a rhumba troupe and coming down the walk, what I can only call mummers having no knowledge of the lore behind the costumes and rhythm. This is truly beyond what I could have imagined.

Too soon it is ending. We finish up in the courtyard listening to a band that has a life and a joi de vivre that seems boundless. The music is sexual and sensual and all though I do not understand the language, it speaks to me still. People dance in the crowd with a certain abandon. In Cuba, where there is music, there is dancing.

Tomorrow will soon be on us and we must know where to go and what to do. Things seem be just a bit up in the air. We question those around us and learn that in spite of tonight, the busses do come to the Parque Central. It's Cuba.

Wednesday, February 27, 2013 – Blank stares and possibilities.

I am awoken by a most disturbing noise and accompanying revelation. The chicken is a rooster. The rooster's crow is interrupted by a cacophony of terrified bird noises and frantic flapping of wings. I think the peacock is raping the rooster. As I leave the hotel, stepping carefully, I notice a few feathers strewn across the floor.

Today we head for Pinar Del Rio on a tobacco farm tour. It is a 2 hour journey to reach our destination. We arrive early at the Parque Central Hotel and enter the lobby which is also a bar/restaurant. We were told that the busses would arrive at

7:00am so we were there early wishing not to miss our first event. "What fools these mortals be". Having missed breakfast in our hotel because they do not serve that early in spite of the fact that we had requested an early feeding and were told that it would be no problem, Ioannis spies a bakery on our walk and darts in to purchase a bun for each of us. I am sure that we have become legend in Havana for having paid the highest price for a single bun in recorded history.

We arrive at the Central and see no busses. There are no Habanos officials and absolutely no indication that this is an official hotel for the festival. Undaunted, we enter the hotel. Ioannis, and he will become a master and my savior in this, takes the initiative to inquire about the busses and the festival. I watch him as he first approaches a member of the lobby staff, then the concierge and finally the main desk to determine if we are in the right place at the right time. The responses? Blank stares. Information was more than a scarce commodity, it was golden and all were flat broke.

I had a sense of foreboding that I cannot quite identify. Ioannis and I have agreed to be positive and optimistic in all things. For every blank stare there is an opportunity. When a door closes a window opens. We will be rewarded with believing that should one thing fail another will supplant and succeed. This is Cuba and that is life. Shit happens.

We order coffees and wait while the table across from us orders mojitos and rum. We discuss the possibilities of the order being the end of a long night or the beginning of a short day. Hard to tell.

Time runs on and we decide to wait on the sidewalk. Just in case, Ioannis inquires yet again about the busses and again he harvests blank stares. This will become the crop of the week. Blank stares. It's Cuba.

Others begin to join us on the street. We speak and learn that they are brothers and sister of the blank stare as well. A small dog, of which there are a phenomenal number, defends his rights to the corner we occupy by chasing off an interloper. I suddenly notice the piss stains on all the pillars and the turds on the sidewalk and make a mental note. Watch your step in the streets as well, it's Paris rules on cleaning up after your dog. In truth I believe that most of them are feral and what I think of as snack food for my giant malamutes back home. Most of them sport welts, wounds and lesions. I do not pet them.

More expectant bus riders join us and we become a herd. Critical mass is a possibility. We were told 7:00 a.m. but it now approaches 8. We are not the only ones to receive bank stares. Where are the busses?

The assemblage on the curb is quite diverse. It is a virtual United Nations of cultures. This will prove problematic in the hours to come. Tourist herds of mixed ethnicity can create chaos as each culture has its own herding protocol there can be a struggle for dominance and a clash of dogma. I will not provide details but suffice it to say, things got pretty ugly. Some would require a great deal of information and history, asking endless questions, others would wander off or not return to the bus on time causing the B grade horror come slasher movie effect where person after person is sent off to find the lost individual and is subsequently slain by the villain or alien creature. There were those who were of the high maintenance variety, ones that preferred regiment, pushers and queue jumpers and three that got off the bus and pissed by the side of the road when we stopped to pick up refugees from another bus that had broken down.

But I have now given away the mystery, obviously the bus did arrive. Sometime just prior to 8:30 the Transtur vehicle trundled to a stop at the curb side and our tour guide stepped down and onto the street wearing a blank stare. This is Wolfgang. Hardly a Cuban name to say the least. His parents liked classical music it seemed.

We were herded onto the bus where we waited for the inevitable late arrivals and Wolfgang sorted out who had tickets, who did not and did it really matter. This was accomplished in three different languages. Linguistics turned out to be his only skill.

Brief stops at two other hotels, distribution of free straw hats, a bottle of tuKola (don't ask) and the Cuban version of a Twinkie and our two hour journey to Pinar del Rio is underway. Wolfgang gives us an abbreviated rundown of the day explaining he has no idea what is going to happen until we get there. We also learn that Wolfie is not a cigar smoker and knows nothing about tobacco or farming. This is going to be difficult, in three different languages.

The day is disjointed. We first visit a sorting plant, then a facility that ages, ferments, prepares and packages the tobacco for shipping and finally a farm where the process actually begins. We are bombarded with information from our guides at each stop as translated by Wolfgang into three different languages. At the farm we receive what turns out to be a pre-lunch of water and buns with a ridiculous amount of butter and some sort of meat product with cheese. Then we are taken for lunch which we thought we had eaten disappointedly at the farm.

Lunch is at an outdoor disco or night club just east of Pinar del Rio, which is a city as well as a province. A free cigar (two for some people), tickets for two drinks and a meal. I missed the second cigar because I had to have my first bowel movement since leaving home. It was way better than any free cigar could have been. Wolfgang has been pressing our group to hurry so we can get back in time for those who are attending the party at the old Partagas factory in the evening. On the bus we wait for the inevitable stragglers. Prior to leaving, Wolfgang tells us that he has conferred with some of the Habanos officials and he has been told that the party at the Partagas factory has been cancelled and the factory tour has been moved to tomorrow (Thursday) instead of Friday. This makes little or no sense. It turns out to be a mistake. It's Cuba.

On the trip back to Havana, we see a car that has back ended a truck. They have no insurance here. You pay for your own repairs. They also have no car dealerships as well. A twenty year old Lada sells for 10,000 CUC if someone can afford to buy it. We rescue the remaining passengers from the broken down bus and the French contingent pisses by the side of the road. We all agree not to shake hands with them.

As we travel what is a freeway, there are people that stand precariously close to the traffic waiting for transport or signally to passing traffic with the wave of a hand that they require a lift. Transport ranges from a horse and buggy arrangement, to small flat-decks with school bus bodies welded to them, to pickup trucks and semi-trailers modified to carry people. I even witnessed a dump truck full of heads travelling in the opposite direction.

Oxen are still used to till the earth. I see only two tractors during the course of our day. Beef is mostly served to tourists in spite of the fact that cattle proliferate in the landscape. The

Cubans believe that there is not enough to go around for everyone. Goats seem pretty popular. Industrialized farming and a bit of technology would be a good thing here. They import 80% of their produce.

Where those of us from many western cultures are used to billboards that advertise McDonalds or Motel 6, in Cuba they extoll the virtues of the revolution and its continuing benefits to the country. Faces of Che and Fidel are everywhere. Signs and state sponsored Graffiti litter flat surfaces. I see an old woman pinning cardboard signs of support for the revolution on a chain link fence. Support for the Communists seems strongest in rural society. The farmers may have benefitted the most. Those I have spoken to in Havana have a different attitude. They would like change. They want the internet, smart phones and Apple. They do have some of that now but they are three or four generations behind. My cell phone is off and Wi-Fi is not an option in my hotel.

This excursion has allowed me to get to know my incidental companion, Ioannis, a little better. He is twenty years my junior, a doctor and Greek by birth but residing in London. We seem to get along and enjoy private jokes at the expense of the herd. He is bright and well-read with a sense of humor I can appreciate and a laugh that is quick and honest. I will grow to feel lucky that he is the one I have been paired with. I will miss his companionship when he leaves two days before me. Generally, I travel alone because I dislike the commitment of others but I find our time together to be simple and easy. I swear like a truck driver yet I do not recall him ever using an expletive although he claims otherwise.

We also make the companionship of two Americans originally from New York. As a Canadian, I am compelled to certain contempt towards those that are south of our border but this father and son duo turn out to be most entertaining. We will all become friends, or at least form some strange sort of alliance. They had a relationship as father and son that I could only be jealous of. We thought at first they were only buddies it was so good. Josh, the son, turned out to be a font of knowledge, a man of action and a fixer supreme. I would love to have the cajounes he displayed in walking up to the crowd of Cubans in the park and announcing his support of the Mets. Baseball is a religion in Cuba. Both father and son display Cuban flags at their homes, one within sight of the capitol in DC.

The remainder of our trip is passed in mostly quiet conversation or sleep interrupted by announcements, reminders to tip the tour guide, answers and blank stares from Wolfgang in three different languages. We look forward to possibilities and the truth about the factory tours. Later, two private functions but first, a cigar.

After a brief respite and change of clothing, Ioannis and I meet later in the lobby and walk to the taxi stand where he is delighted to learn that we would be travelling to our first destination in a Lada. This will not be our last encounter with this transport of infamy.

We are taken to the Hotel Nacional. This is a building of history both grand and notorious. It was the location used in The Godfather Pt. 2 but also entertained the likes of Lucky Luciano and Meyer Lansky. Built in 1930, it was once a casino operated by the mob which Castro closed in 1960. Fidel Castro and Che Guevara set up their headquarters here to prepare the defense of Havana from aerial attack. It is now a grand institution and mecca for tourists. The lobby and grounds are elegant and speak of glamour long since passed. It hosted such guests as Frank Sinatra, Ava Gardner, Mickey Mantle, Rocky

Marciano, Tyrone Power, Errol Flynn, John Wayne, Marlene Dietrich, Gary Cooper, Marlon Brando and Ernest Hemingway. In 1956, Nat King Cole was contracted to perform here but disallowed residence because he was black.

We are met at the entrance to the 1930 Ballroom by an Arabian gentleman in full traditional dress. He is an artist displaying and selling his work and is providing each quest with a "Hello I'm …" card with your name written in Arabic.

There is a replica humidor of the hotel that is four or five feet wide and at least three feet in height and depth. It is exact down to the finest detail and filled with between 350 and 500 cigars. It sells at auction for $31,000.00 CUC. We are handed cigars, a lighter, a cutter and a keychain with a fob made from tobacco to look like a leaf. Later I receive a rose from Michael's wife Vivienne that has also been made from tobacco. There is music, dancing and rum. Everything is free.

 An hour or so later we leave to attend another party at the Old Partagas Factory which is now a museum. This is the event that Wolfgang told us was cancelled. The Factory tours would also not be the next day but on Friday as scheduled. We were prepared with other opportunities should that not have been the case. Everything works out, one way or another.

The Old Partagas Factory sits behind the National Capital building which resembles the US Capitol in Washington. The factory no longer produces cigars but instead pays homage to the cigar industry as a museum. Museums are very popular in Havana and if you come up with an interest, there will be a museum to inform you about it.

This turns out to be the best of all the private functions we attend. It is crowded and hot and full of smoke. The party is contained to a hallway, the cigar shop and a gallery. The music

126

is pulsing and people dance among the crowd. There are auctions, raffles, mojitos and cigars. There are humidors on display for sale that defy imagination. These are works of art. The shop and smoking lounge are packed. The crowd is diverse. Ioannis and I spy a very tall woman dressed in black. Her makeup is dramatic with jewelry to match. She smokes a petite corona and seems to be entertaining the gentleman she stands with. We speculate that she is Russian and undoubtedly a spy or assassin. Her name must be Svetlana. We are certain that in the morning, the man she is speaking to will turn up dead in his hotel room.

The party does not end, it just seems to slowly fade from reality. It is late, I am exhausted, sweat soaked and we have a bit of a walk back to our hotel. We have made arrangements with Michael to meet us at the exhibition at 10:30 am the next day. He will get us passes and be waiting at the bottom of the stairs that lead to the exhibition floor. I throw caution and Murphy's' law to the wind and urge Michael to be there on time. This is Cuba after all.

We will arrive an hour late. Michael was on time.

Thursday, February 28, 2013 – Peacocks and Tickets and Cruising the Malecon

It is raining. I sit after breakfast enjoying a cigar and some Cuban coffee. As I work on my journal I realize that these must be the most uncomfortable chairs I have ever sat in. Marcel, the peacock vacillates between games of harass the guests and torment the younger male peacock by chasing him about the hotel. The Conde de Villanueva is an historic sight and on the list of visits for every tourist herd roaming old Havana. I avoid the temptation to behave like an animal on display in a zoo. I warn no one of the ornery peacock and watch as Marcel draws victims within reach by displaying his shaggy and sparse tail feathers. I smile as I watch peacock shit being scraped from shoes.

Ioannis comes by and we decide to try and wait out the rain before going to the exhibition. In Vancouver we would call it high humidity or perhaps heavy dew but here it is rain. We meet shortly after 10:00 and wait but the weather does not change so reluctantly I don my golf jacket and Ioannis pops a bumby and we leave.

Michael is not at the appointed meeting place because we are an hour late. After a bit of negotiation we manage to purchase entrance to the show. We are quickly separated and Ioannis is nowhere to be found. I strongly suspect that he is off trying to bargain his way into the tobacco gastronomy seminar.

I wander the floor where there are booths full of antique cigar memorabilia. More irony still as I spy a zippo lighter emblazoned with the iconic face of Che cradled in a box which proudly states; "Made in the USA". I come across the shop belonging to the man whose collection we were to visit but had been dropped from our itinerary. It's Cuba. I purchase a metal cigar sign circa 1920 for my club back home. It is rusted and fragile but rare and unique. There is clothing (mostly guayaberas) and figurines and more fascinating humidors. There are antiques and artwork everywhere but for the most part they are overpriced. I give in and buy a fine linen guayabera then search for Ioannis but find Michael instead. I am certain he's at least a little put out. He had been waiting for us and purchased tickets for us that he would now have to return. I express my apologies and he tells me he is working on getting us tickets to the Vigueros dinner that evening. It is another event that fell from our itinerary. He has not seen Ioannis either.

More wandering and searching and bumping into Michael who has found one ticket for the evening and what would we like to do should he not find another and what about the show at the Tropicana? We agree to be in contact at some point somehow after I confer with Ioannis. Shortly after we part company I come across my compatriot just released from a tobacco gastronomy seminar. He fills me in on all things foodie infused with tobacco. I resolve to smoke it instead.

We talk and agree that the exhibition is not quite what we expected. This is a Casa del Habanos sponsored event so the individual brands are represented under the umbrella of Habanos. The only free cigars to be had are one machine rolled panatela no thicker than a pencil and a fresh hand rolled one that requires permission from the floor director to obtain. After a game of tag with several staffers Ioannis secures us the permission to receive a hand rolled cigar and we arrive at his station just in time for his lunch break. We leave.

Back at our hotel, a phone call to Michael and he has obtained tickets to the dinner. Our original itinerary has not only been fully restored but augmented beyond our expectations. It's Cuba. Michael will be coming by around 3:00 so we go the Lamparilla.

As I have said, service is not a well-developed concept in Cuba. It is mostly slow and inattentive. Don't bother trying to send back an underdone piece of meat because your request will be met with a blank stare. Order everything well done and hope for the best. After perusing the menu we opt for two appetizers and mains. The first appetizer has been listed in English as "Tuffed Potatoes" and after speculating what a tuffed potato might be we also chose a malanga fritter which we will learn is a staple on almost every menu. The malanga will become the brunt of many jokes to come.

"The Malanga root has a tough brown and shaggy patchy thin skin that reveals its reddish, beige or yellowish flesh. Not consistent in shape, some are long while others are curvy, usually weighing in about one-half to two pounds. The flesh varies as well and may be pinkish, cream-colored or yellow. Cooked Malanga delivers a distinct nutlike flavor and texture. Boiled Malanga develops a unique smooth melting quality."

As it turns out, the tuffed potato is actually a blended mash of malanga with sundry other bits of produce, spices and possibly meat. It arrives at our table with two on a plate bringing to mind the head on a platter expression utilizing a different portion of the anatomy. They are dark brown, breaded, pan fried and about the size of a tennis ball. They taste like an entire leftover turkey dinner including the gravy. They remain partially eaten while we wait for our second starter. It would appear that you do not get your next plate until the first has been finished. As we had not cleaned our plate no fritters were forthcoming. After managing to attract the attention of a meandering waiter and explaining that we were done with the tuffed potatoes, the dish was removed along with a blank stare.

The fritters are delivered. Mashed malanga in the shape of a football (American), deep fried and eight on the plate. They are battered and obviously overcooked. What have we done? Undaunted, we dig in, then spit. They taste so strongly of old fishy oil that it is an impossibility to tell if the internal ingredients are worth the effort of chewing. The conundrum we face is that if we do not make them disappear there is the chance that we may never see our mains. Fortunately, the outdoor seating provides many potted plants surrounding the dining area.

This would not be the last time we encountered the dreaded malanga potato balls. They showed up at every turn, on every menu and appetizer plate that circled the parties.

I believe we are both fearing the entrees. Neither of us expresses our trepidation but the air is fraught with dreaded anticipation. It is Cuba, the mains were fine. My grilled lobster had some sort of cheese product melted on the top but it did not detract from the flavor. The veg consists of sautéed carrots, peppers and cabbage. Another menu staple.

Back to the hotel to meet Michael and enjoy another Cuban cigar. He arrives with the tickets and the resident cigar roller pops by our table to drop off a few fresh and free ones.

For the first time in what seems like days (it has been days) I have the time for a nap. I take full advantage in an attempt to make up for the sleep I have lost.

We take a taxi out to the convention center for the Vigueros dinner. This is an old manufacturer that is trying to resurrect itself with the launch of a new line of cigars. Not quite the spectacle of the opening night but a respectable display nonetheless. The staff are bedecked in costumes with colors that match the packing of the brand. This night is in honor of the farmers and guayaberas are the mode of dress. There is a group of some thirty odd Canadians all dressed in red ones. I must have missed the memo. I wore my black club shirt. I tried to introduce myself to all the tables where the Canadians were seated but was soon snubbed when I revealed that I purchased my cigars online instead of at one of their shops in spite of the fact that not a one was from Vancouver.

We were handed a small selection of the new wares with yet another cutter and lighter. A different cigar appeared with each course of dinner. Another night of excessive consumption. It would seem that Casa del Habanos understands very well the value of promotion and spares no expense in taking good care of their clients. A 465 million dollar net profit will do that.

There were a few speeches and other such formalities before dinner was served and the entertainment took to the stage. More Latino passion put to rhythm and lyrics. The music is infectious. We are seated at a table of representatives from Venezuela and Argentina or some other South American country. Our late tickets have us sitting far from the stage. Our American friends from the farm tour are at the table next to ours. We exchange greetings and spend much of the night table hopping. One of the gentlemen from South America lights up a cigar so large that it is clear he is compensating for some other deficiency. Those on either side of him duck as he turns his head from side to side with the cigar wedged between his teeth. The food is quite good but the new cigars are young and need time to mature. The last cigar of the evening, delivered with dessert is by far the star of the night.

Soon it is beyond midnight and we head from the hall joining with the Americans to avoid the busses provided and hire a 55 Chevy to cruise down the Malecon and head for the Mezzanine Bar of the Saratoga Hotel. The bar boasts a beautiful mural by Cuban painter Juan Carlos Botello and is open 24 hours a day. We have our picture taken as a group behind the bar then smoke and talk well into the morning. Josh regales us with stories and facts. He is truly an encyclopedia of Cuban history and a master conversationalist. Philosophy, politics and opinion flood the room.

At 3:00 am I finally slip into bed. We have to be on the bus at 8:00 for the factory tour.

Friday, March 1, 2013 – Cigar Sharks, Adios Americanos and the Tropicana

Another morning too early and yet too late for much more than a coffee and some fruit. Just as well, I am too tired to chew.

Back to the Parque Central where we sit in the lobby with Josh and his father and wait for the 8:00 busses that show up at 8:45. Wolfgang returns. I have forgotten my ticket but this never materializes as an issue. We will be visiting only one factory not two as the itinerary had implied. At the Partagas factory (the working one) it is quietly disclosed that we can chose between this one and the Upman factory around the corner. Ioannis and I opt for the Partagas factory while the Americans went off to the other. We opted poorly as it turned out. We had been told earlier at the opening night festivities by one of my countryman, that it is possible to purchase cigars from the rollers in the factories if done surreptitiously. Be prepared with money and deep pockets.

The Partagas factory was locked down tighter than a Maximum Security prison in Texas. The tour was brief but interesting. Another free cigar as we left. On the street, we gather and wait for stragglers. Returning around the corner we see Josh and his father. Josh carries a white plastic shopping bag and a smile that would make a Cheshire cat jealous. He is a school boy returning on Halloween night with a bag full of treats. "Look at this" he exclaims opening the bag to show us his booty. The bag was half full of labelled cigars purchased at a discount directly from the table they were rolled on.

A faster start to an Olympic sprint would only rival the race that began to the Upman factory by all those within earshot or sightline who had just exited the Partagas shop. The ensuing

133

scene in the dubious rolling room resembled a feeding frenzy displayed by starving sharks amid a school of unfortunate fish.

Pockets bulging with under the counter merchandise, we shrugged the bus ride back on Josh's insistence that a short walk, just around the corner and we would arrive at a favorite haunt of his. What I have learned is a typical trait of New Yorkers, is to dramatically underestimate the distance of a journey. In Manhattan, the Battery is just around the corner from Central Park (a distance better calculated in miles). I failed to take this into account when agreeing to forgo a taxi and walk to our next destination. A 45 minute trek brought us to the closed doors of our intended destination. The solution? Coconut ice cream served on the half shell. It was delightful.

Off to a local cigar lounge for a smoke and cheese with bread. This would be our last encounter with the Americans. Time well spent that did more to improve U.S./Canadian relations than the Reciprocity Treaty of 1854.

Goodbyes and the exchange of emails left Ioannis and I on the rainy street heading for La Guarida, a recommended paladare, for lunch. We threw all caution to the wind and hired a Pedi cab for the 8 block trip. To put it delicately, I am a man of size and the fellow that was to pedal us to La Guarida could not have weighed much more than my left leg. He earned his generous tip. It was our intent to avoid getting wet by travelling in a covered pedal powered rickshaw but it was a dream to expect such an outcome. The roof (and I use that term loosely) was a tailored tarpaulin lashed to a spider web frame work of 3/8 inch steel concrete reinforcing bar. The seating was narrow but just wide enough to leave both of us half exposed to the elements. I dared not inspect the construction of the bicycle portion for fear of fear itself as we weave through the Havana traffic where vehicles of this nature and pedestrians are considered targets of opportunity.

La Guarida resided at the top of a three story walk up. The building at one time could have been grand but was now in such a state of decay and disrepair that it barely hung on to the term "charming". A statue that made "Venus de Milo" look gifted in terms of appendages stood alongside a winding marble staircase girdled with wrought iron and a haggard marble hand rail. The paladare at the top could very well have been an apartment at one time. A small reception hall allowed guests an open view into the kitchen and there were several small rooms scattered about for diners to sit at tables surrounded by an eclectic arrangement of chairs, no two of which matched. It was a Hodgepodge of design and décor that could have existed in any village or plaza on the Mediterranean. The food was quite good and the service attentive. Were we still in Havana? Not for the time being.

Still raining after lunch we managed to survive the ride back to our hotel in yet another Lada, this one constructed by Dr. Frankenstein himself. No lining on the roof, half a dashboard that contained what appeared to be a cassette tape deck, a passenger door with no panel that was wired shut, back seats reminiscent of an old sofa (probably was) and when I leaned back, a leak in the rear window. It's Cuba.

We purchased tickets for the show at the Tropicana in the Ambos Mundos Hotel. Hemingway stayed and wrote one of his novels here. Where we may be used to the likes of Ticketmaster, here there are handwritten forms and phone calls required to confirm our reservation. Organizational communications and skills are not what we are used to.

The Tropicana show starts at 10:00 so we fill in the wait attending parties at the Habana Libré and Milia Cohiba hotels. More abundance of food, beverages, cigars and entertainment. There is a fashion show at the Milia Cohiba with tall, dark models holding unlit cigars wearing Cuban Haute Couture providing the backdrop for more auctions and raffles of unique humidors and cigars. I have reached my limit. The celebrations have become a blur.

But now, on to the Tropicana. Billed as a Las Vegas style review it is an institution and must see for any visitor to Havana. Arriving by taxi, the driveway evokes images of Mafia run Las Vegas. I wouldn't be surprised to see the Rat Pack give an impromptu performance. This is a scene from a Hollywood movie set late in the fifties or early sixties. Ioannis negotiates us a better table at the edge of the stage and following the entre act performance of a string octet playing well arranged standards plus an eerily appropriate rendition of the theme from The Godfather, the show begins.

Big band Latin music reminiscent of Xavier Cugat or Desi Arnaz accompanies singers and dancers dressed in bright Caribbean attire. Not quite a variety review, it features mostly large and diverse dance numbers interspersed with solos and duets and a couple circus type acts worthy of the Ed Sullivan Show. At one point, several girls of the chorus enter the stage wearing what can only be chandeliers on their heads. There is a Romeo and Juliet tribal dance number and an over the top finale.

As a performer myself, I watch with a critical eye whether I like it or not. The dancers shoes are worn, the costumes a bit tired, the choreography all too much alike and the performers may have been doing this show a bit too long. But this is not Broadway or Las Vegas so sit back and enjoy the ambience and the show in spite of its minor flaws. Much like my hotel, it is perfect in its own way.

Saturday, March 2, 2013 – Too Tired to Think of a Title

On the last night the Cigar Festival concluded with a formal Gala Dinner. I did not attend as I simply could not justify the $550.00 cost. I will never know.

I awake searching for the wheels that have finally come off my party wagon. I am totally exhausted. Spent. It is both disconcerting and immensely satisfying at the same time.

Ioannis is leaving today and has some purchases to make before he goes so I join him for a final day in Havana. As we step from the hotel, a man carrying a stack of plastic hangers and a bucket full of rags dressed rather shabbily in jean shorts and a dirty t-shirt asks if we are interested in a woman. He is the most unlikely pimp I have ever seen.

On the way to the Partagas Factory store we meet a young Cuban couple on their way to a salsa festival. One thing leads to another and he tells us he is part of a co-operative of cigar factory workers that save their daily quota of cigars to sell on the streets at a discount. The pitch is good and we succumb. After a short walk through the streets while the young women tells me of rationing, traffic, music and the difficulties of life in Cuba, we enter a small Cuban home. The door opens up directly off the street. There are very few rooms and they are cramped with old furniture and a television set I would give away back home.

A young girl lies on the couch covered with a blanket and looks up to me blinking and smiling coming out of an afternoon nap. In the kitchen, more a term of reference than a description, on the table sit boxes of Cuban cigars. I am not an expert but I have a pretty good idea of what a fake should look like and these looked good. The young man makes his pitch like a master. I inspect and look and sniff and check the labels and the quality of the roll and if these are not real then they are the best fauxhibas I have ever seen. The boxes even carry the Habanos hologram. After haggling and bargaining we both make a purchase in spite of all the warnings not to do so but I can say the cigars that I bought were certainly Cuban and smoked very well. As we leave out the back through what once may have been a courtyard the young women becomes sad eyed and reminds me of how hard life is in Cuba particularly for her baby. Contrary to my skeptical feelings and believing this may be no more than a come on, I give her some money to help her out. At the end of the day, I have so much and so many here have so little, that all conning aside, I didn't mind in the least.

After a stop at Partagas, we drop into La Floridita, a restaurant and bar where, according to legend, the daiquiri was born. The menus, some plaques and the writing on the wall all proclaim this to be the "Cradle of the Daiquiri" and Hemmingway's second home. A bronze statue in the corner of the man himself attracts more attention and photographs than the band that plays amazing tunes from the small stage near the door. Tourists jostle and shuffle to stand with their arm about the shoulder of the bronze author and smile at the camera for all the folks back home. If they could only click the shutters on their cameras in time to the beat then they could join the musicians they hide from our view.

We have just enough time left for a quick lunch at the paladare across the street from our hotel. The Paladare de Mercaderes sits on the second floor overlooking the street. It could be a small French bistro if it wanted. Unlike La Guarida, a great deal more care and attention has been taken in its entire decor. A trio stands on the balcony waiting for the stimulus to play. I drop enough CUC in their plate to urge them to play right through our lunch which turns out to be excellent. There is a myth that the food in Cuba is not very good but my experience is that just like everywhere else, you simply have to know where to eat.

There is nothing left on my itinerary other than to make a few purchases for my family. Never come home empty handed. I hang around the courtyard enjoying yet another free cigar and conversation with some fellow Canadians until Ioannis comes down on his way home. We agree that we have been lucky to be partners in this adventure and exchange email addresses. It all seems a bit different after he leaves. We have shared something not unique but certainly rare that comes along few times in your life.

I dine in the hotel, house paella containing unshelled shrimp and a couple large pieces of mystery meat. It's filling. The staff is now calling me Hemmingway and I am greeted with the traditional Cuban handshake of slapping hands together brought down from shoulder height, grasping firmly and shaking with authority. Some call me "mi amigo". The service may not be the best but never have I felt the honest sense of friendship and warmth from the staff of any establishment I have occupied more than here.

Sunday, March 3, 2013 – Last Day in Havana

My last day in Havana. I try to sleep in but fail. My mission for the day is to walk to the craft and souvenir market in the harbor and search for appropriate gifts. First a stop at the Cadeca (or Casas de Cambio) which is a money exchange and a stop I have made a few times this week. The lineup is long which seems usual and leads me to believe that there is a lot of money coming into Cuba.

The market resides in a large old warehouse on the edge of the harbor and is filled with booths and aisles of mostly trash and trinkets designed for tourist consumption. I am reminded of night markets in Thailand. It is a haven of free enterprise in a communist country. Not all the booths are filled with t-shirts, ceramics, hats or toys. There is a massive display of paintings, photos and sketches that range from scenes of old Havana that depict the Chevy and Che motif to abstracts and still lives that mimic and mock some well-known artists. It is mind numbing trying to choose one for my wife. I wander for what must be 2 hours and finally make my selections of a shot glass, a t-shirt, a couple of fashionable Cuban military hats and a painted acrylic scene of the Pinar del Rio region of Cuba. Victorious and smug, I head back to my hotel through the old brothel district of Havana.

I purchase my allotment of cigars from the shop in the hotel and have lunch at La Imprenta where my 400 gram fillet (nearly 1 lb.) which I ordered medium rare shows up at my table well grilled on the outside but leaving me feel as though they had ripped the horns off and thrown it on the plate on the inside. Lesson learned.

I spend the rest of my day simply wandering the streets of Old Havana.

It is Sunday and for some reason the streets seem just a bit more alive. There are more huskers and buskers and beggars and invitations for sex than I have experienced all week. School is obviously not in session as there are an abundance of children playing in the streets and plazas. In the Plaza del Cristo young boys have sketched out a small soccer pitch on the cobblestones and play an intense game with a half flat, skinless ball. This scene is repeated with each turn of a corner or stroll down a street. Baseball may be number1 but soccer is a close second.

Suddenly there is a clamor of horns and drums as a bright troupe of stilt walkers and entourage parade up behind me. They are preceded by young women collecting donations in velvet bags hanging on the end of sticks that reach well into the crowd. There are beggars at my arm much too often but soon chased away by the local police. The Cubans are well aware of the value of tourism and it is not to be disturbed.

More street scenes and tableaus and costumed characters and musicians and every other ploy imaginable designed to encourage a CUC from your pocket assail the senses. Somehow, it avoids being obnoxious and becomes a fiesta to be taken in and enjoyed.

Day has become an effortless evening. I take the time to visit each and every member of the staff to say my goodbyes. They all know I will be leaving early in the morning. A taxi has been arranged for 3:30 am to take me to the airport. The woman who has kept the courtyard, lobby and bathrooms impeccably clean takes my hand and wishes me well on my journey and life. She has greeted me each morning with a broad smile and a "hola". I am hugged and thanked and asked to return. They call me Hemmingway and mi amigo and tease me a bit. It all seems genuine and I believe that it is. This is something I have not experienced in any hotel I have stayed at before. I vow to return knowing full well that this may have been a once in a lifetime. It will always remain once in a lifetime should I return or not.

I retire early hoping to get some sleep before my departure. Lying in bed I reflect on the week.

Havana is a city of smiles. It is hard to believe given the hardships but I am reminded by a friend when I get home that when you are all in the same boat then pleasure is found in companionship and simplicity. The pace of life reflects this adage. There is no racing about. In every doorway, someone stands and watches the street. Men stand about on corners and curbs conversing and smoking. People shout from the balconies at friends on the street and everywhere there is music. It comes out of windows and taxis and restaurants and bars and even the Pedi cabs that roam through the streets. It is constant and enduring through the day and the night. It compels you to move, to sway to the rhythm or dance even if you can't.

In spite of its rejuvenation, the city remains timeless with architecture reaching back into centuries past and a drive to catch up to the present. More of the dichotomy that Cuba faces as it lies somewhere between the first and third world of nations, defying definition. The people are friendly and gracious. The streets feel safe, other than the traffic. It is warm and relaxing. It is seductive and vibrant. For all its faults and shortcomings, Havana has been all I could have imagined. It has been perfect and now I must go home.

Monday, March 4, 2013 – Going Home

The phone in my room rings at 3:10 am. My taxi is 20 minutes early. In the end, I couldn't even count on Cuba to be late. We walk to the plaza where the car is parked. It is early. It is dark. I leave Havana in a tarted up Lada with a driver wearing a toque. It is early. It is dark. I leave Havana in a tarted up Lada with a driver wearing a toque.

142

Acknowledgements

I suppose the first acknowledgement goes to life itself for providing some very interesting subject matter.

Thanks to my family. Both as it was and how it is now.

I should also recognize (and perhaps apologize to) all the willing and unwilling participants in my stories.

Thanks to those who laughed and told me I should write a book.

A special thanks to an individual who flattered my ego with praise, told me I should be a writer and provided the encouragement and inspiration to do so. She knows who she is.

Made in the USA
Coppell, TX
26 October 2021